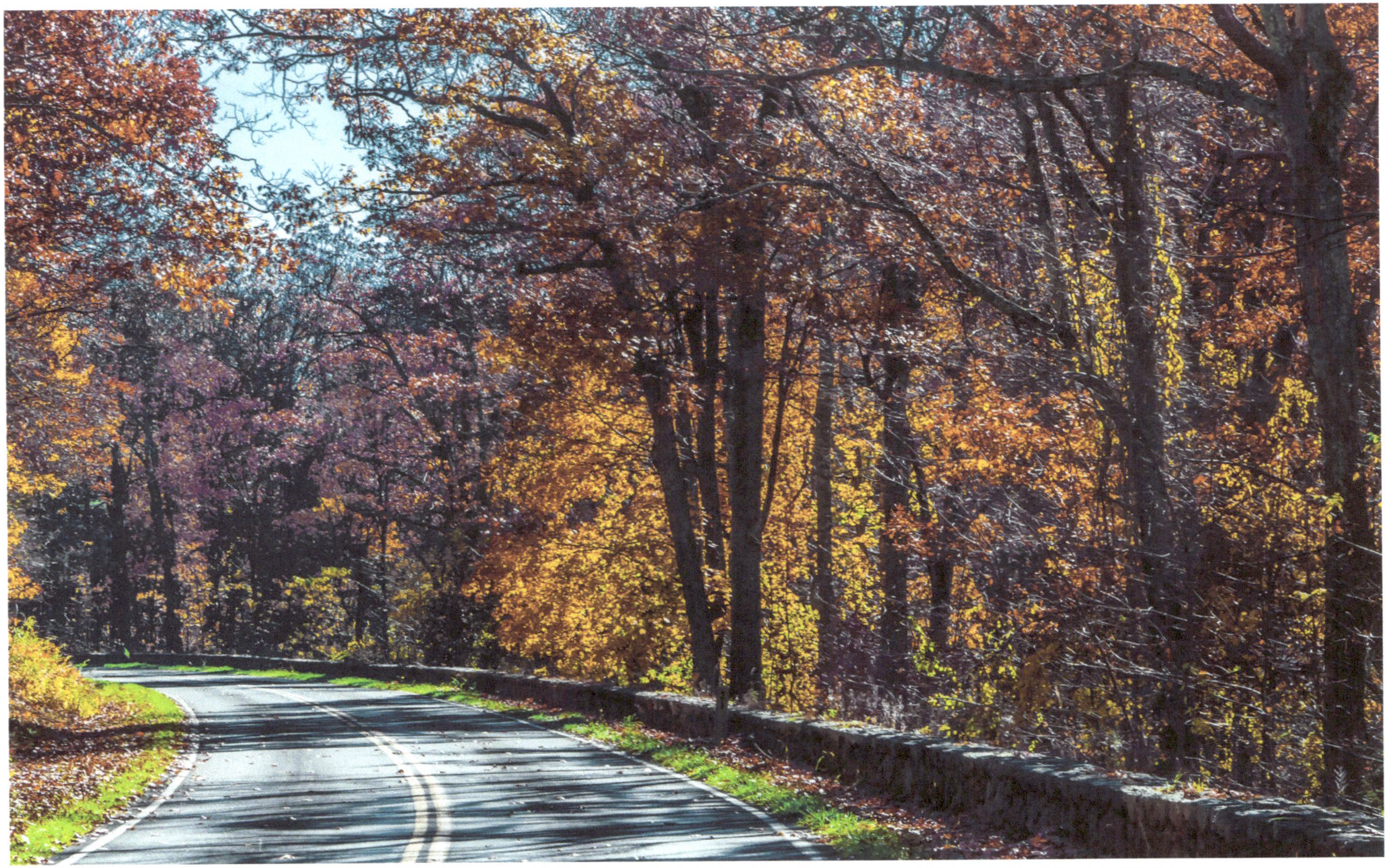

Viewing Fall Foliage from Shenandoah National Park Lookouts

Shirley Nan Washington, Ed.D.

Copyright Page

Copyright 2021 by Shirley Nan Washington

All rights reserved. This book or any portion thereof may not be reproduced or used in any manner whatsoever without the express written permission of the author or publisher.

Preface and Acknowledgments

PREFACE:

Have you ever driven through Virginia's picturesque Shenandoah National Park via Skyline Drive "The Drive" and observed its panoramic views and colorful foliage of the Shenandoah Valley? Are you familiar with the 75 overlooks that provide unique sights from various sides of the mountains, "A View from the Other Side?" Can you visualize standing on a mountaintop and spotting black bears and other wildlife sightings in their natural habitat? Do you enjoy outdoor adventure and recreation? Would you like to meet park rangers and learn more about their ranger programs and interactive exhibits?

This photographic book was created to showcase some of the many spectacular, colorful images the author captured as she traveled the beautiful Skyline Drive, the only public road through Virginia's Shenandoah National Park. Her ten-hour journey was very eventful and tranquil, even when she encountered two black bears. The author drove "The Drive" alone (from Front Royal, Virginia to the Waynesboro-Charlottesville area, 105-miles), on a Wednesday, November 4, 2015. Her purpose was twofold. First, she desired to fulfill a chief entry on her Bucket List. She wanted to re-visit Lewis Mountain, the campgrounds where her father (Gratehouse Robert Washington of Luray, Virginia) drove the family on weekend outings during her childhood. Secondly, she desired to capture countless images of the magnificent views to share with family, friends, and others who enjoy seeing the beauty of the Earth as found in the trees, forests, and wildlife; smelling the fresh air; touching the land and nature, and appreciating nature's sights and sounds.

Although the author aspired to photograph Lewis Mountain Campgrounds, the time element became an issue, for she wanted her mountain trip to end before dark. However, she did photograph more than 60 Lookouts.

ACKNOWLEDGMENTS:

The author wishes to extend her sincere appreciation to two of her Montgomery College professors in Publication Design with InDesign, and Printing Management, for their supervision and encouragement with the production and editing of this third book trilogy about home: Harry St. Ours and William J. Humphrey. In particular, her gratitude also goes to Brian Jones, Coordinator of Photography and to Grace Graham, Photography Instructor, for their photographic image reviews and anecdotal comments; to her college friends, Roger and Raynord, who served in the role of Photography Assistants, and to her sisters, Bernice, Mary Ann and Jean for their continuing support.

About the Author

The author, Shirley Nan Washington, '78 Ed.D. (UMASS), is a native of Harrisonburg, Virginia and resides in Silver Spring, Maryland. She is a retired educator and lifelong learner who is a six-time Montgomery College graduate (with honors) from the following programs of study: Paralegal Studies ('12); Criminal Justice ('13); Photography ('15); Studio Art ('18) General Art ('19) and Communication Studies ('20). Dr. Washington is a recipient of several awards, including: the Dr. Harry Harden Jr. Academic Excellence Student Medallion (2013), the Spirit of Service Medallion for Student Volunteer Service Hours (2016), and Studio Arts Award for Demonstrating Outstanding Academic Performance in the Studio Arts (2019).

Since her undergraduate studies at Virginia State University, Shirley has been actively involved in community affairs and social justice. She holds a Charter Membership in the Smithsonian's National Museum of African American History and Culture and has membership in other organizations, including: ACLU, MSEA and NEA. Her national honor society memberships include Lambda Epsilon Chi (LEX), Phi Delta Kappa, and Phi Theta Kappa. She served 13 years as Ombudsman Representative (volunteer) with the Montgomery County Long Term Care Ombudsman Program (Maryland Enhanced Certification), and she is also a former member of the Wheaton Library Advisory Committee (8 years).

Besides having a great appreciation for the visual arts: capturing photographic images of distinctive sights and sounds, creating works of art, visiting museums, etc., Shirley also enjoys playing the piano, mingling with diverse folks, and learning about drones. She has had photographic and art pieces showcased in juried student exhibitions and in the Sligo Journal.

Shirley reminisces her childhood's love of travel and fascinating art through her vividly dazzling photography. Her three colorful, photographic books showcase road trips' images from some of Virginia's finest and rarest antiques, magnificent arts, unique animals, and scenic views of the Shenandoah Valley and nearby regions. In her 184-page photographic book trilogy, Home, she revisits some of the same Virginia towns she toured as a youngster and shares findings of her picturesque journey.

Introduction

This photographic book contains 46 images of mountain scenery in Virginia's Shenandoah National Park. The images are identified, to the best of the author's knowledge, with the name of the Skyline Drive Overlook and its elevation, and presented by leading lines that create interesting visual narratives.

As you journey with the author, while viewing her photographs, she hopes you will find joy and splendor in the images of the peaceful trees, forests, and other Skyline Drive attractions. She invites you to also consider visiting Virginia's Skyline Drive, especially during the Autumn season when the trees' coloration is vibrant. Finally, she challenges you to share your experiences through writing and publishing a book about the beautiful foliage that showcases your own discovered beauty.

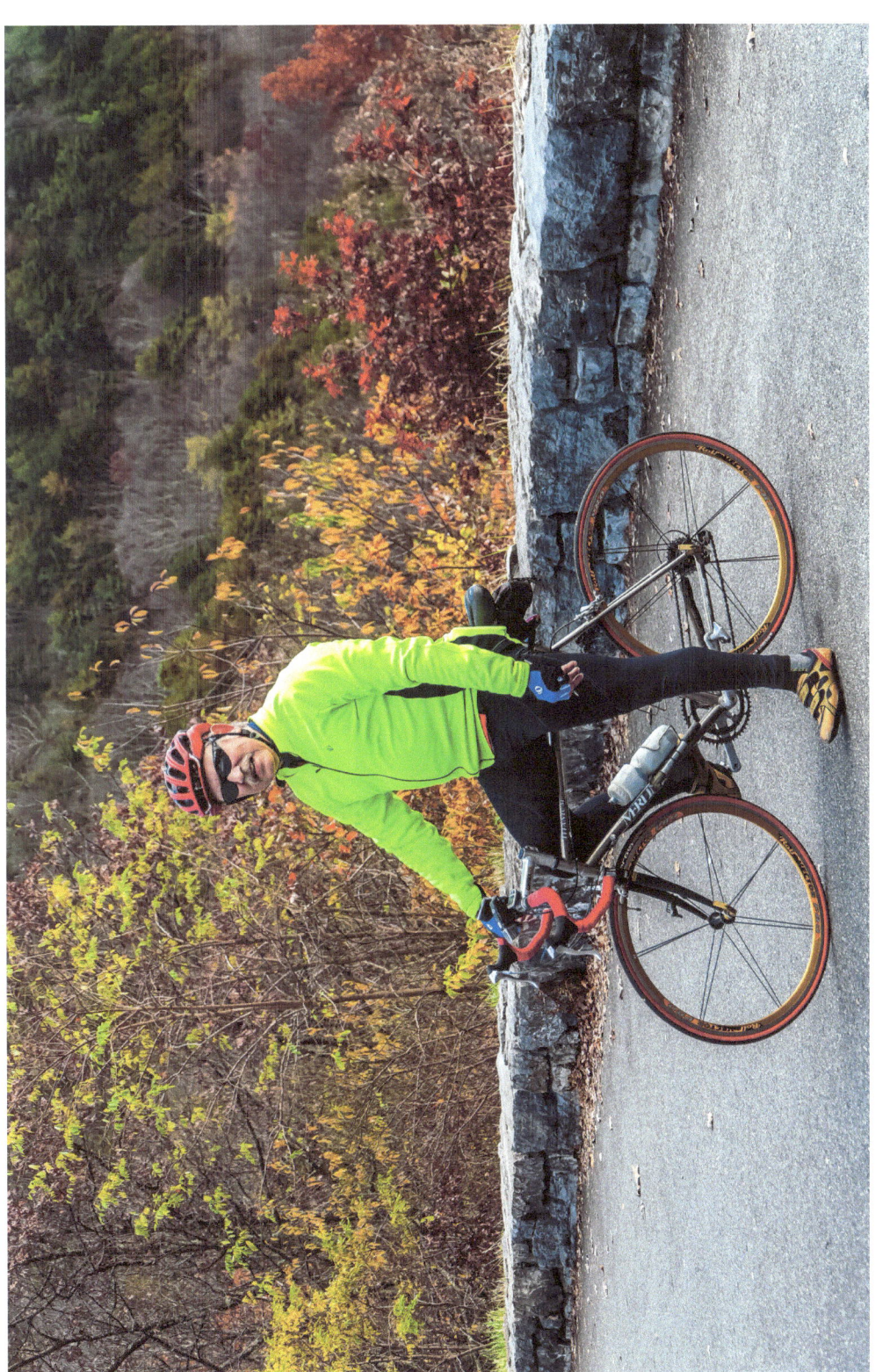

Waynesboro, Virginia Bicyclist - Sawmill Run Overlook (2195 ft.)

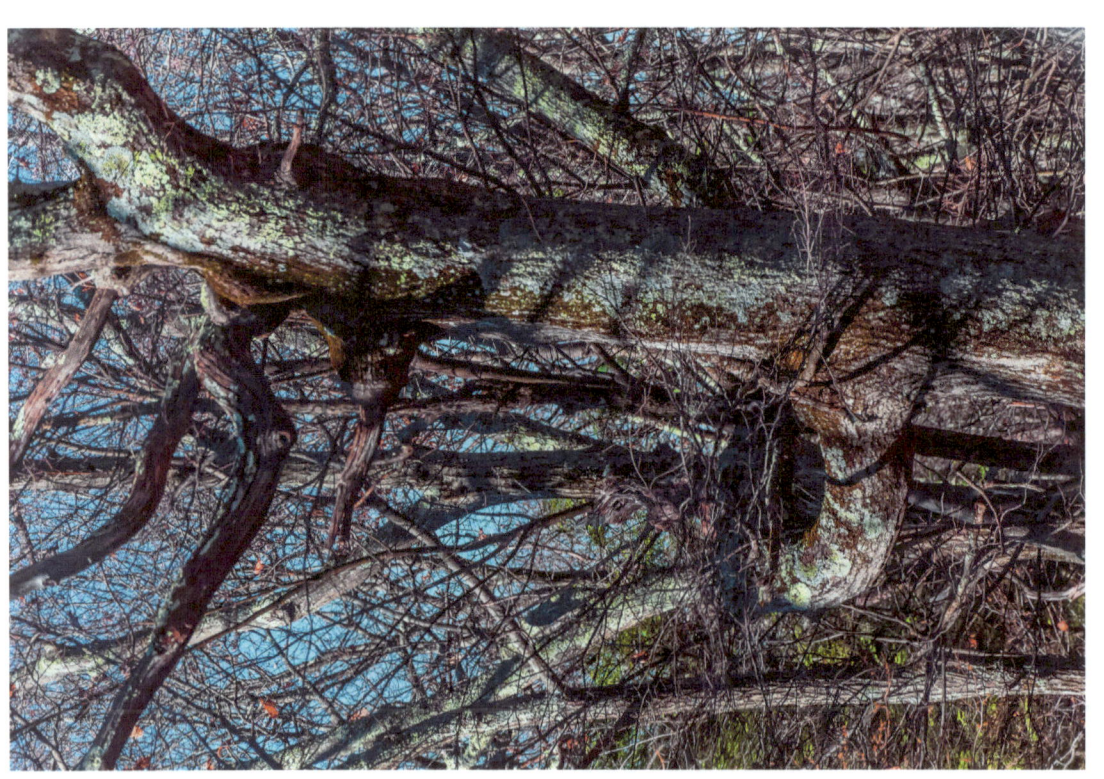

Thick Tree Bark with Growing Moss on Tree
Old Rag View Overlook (3585 ft.)

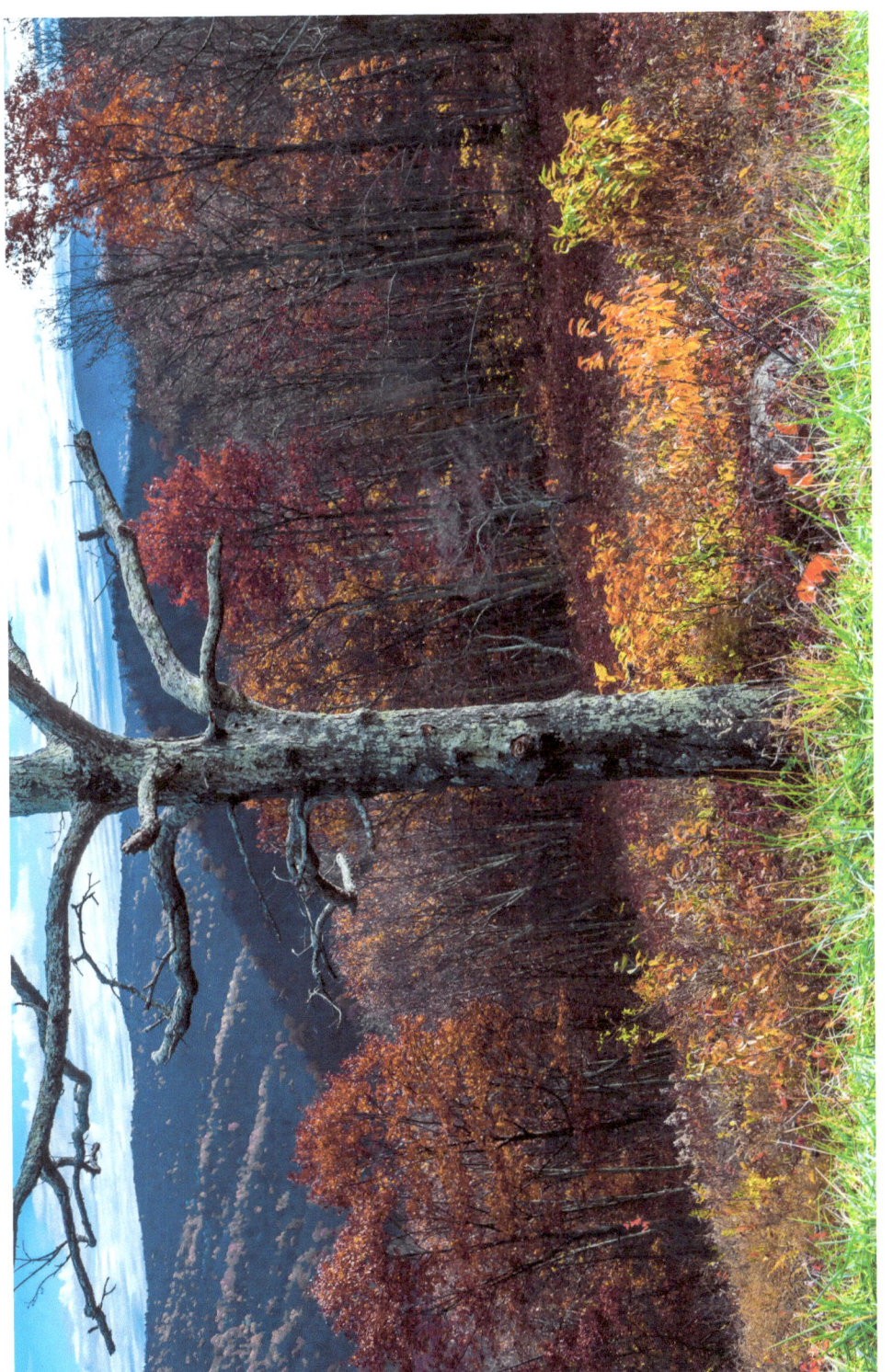

Leafless Tree Among Scenic Landscape 1
Trayfoot Mountain Overlook (2575 ft.)

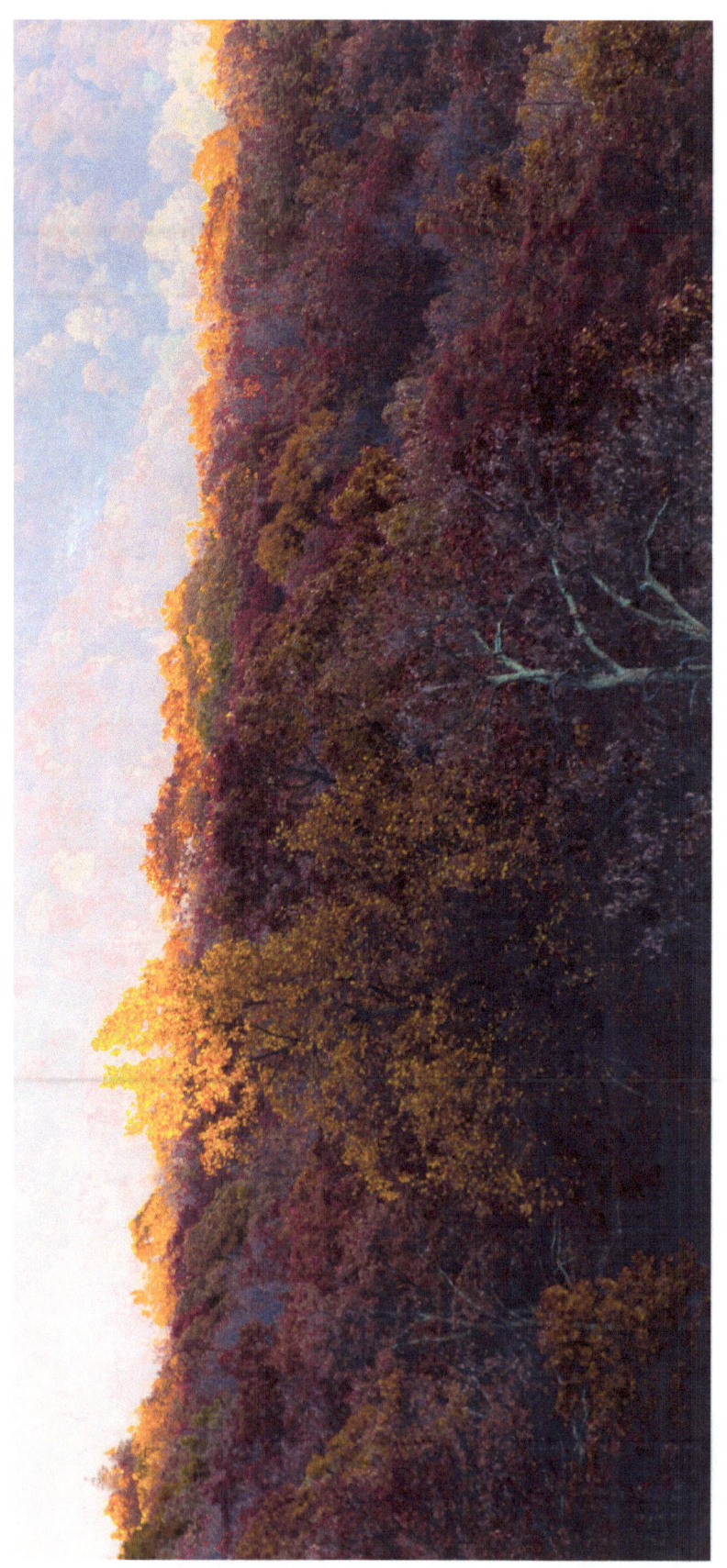

Sunrise Trees - Gooney Run Overlook (2085 ft.)

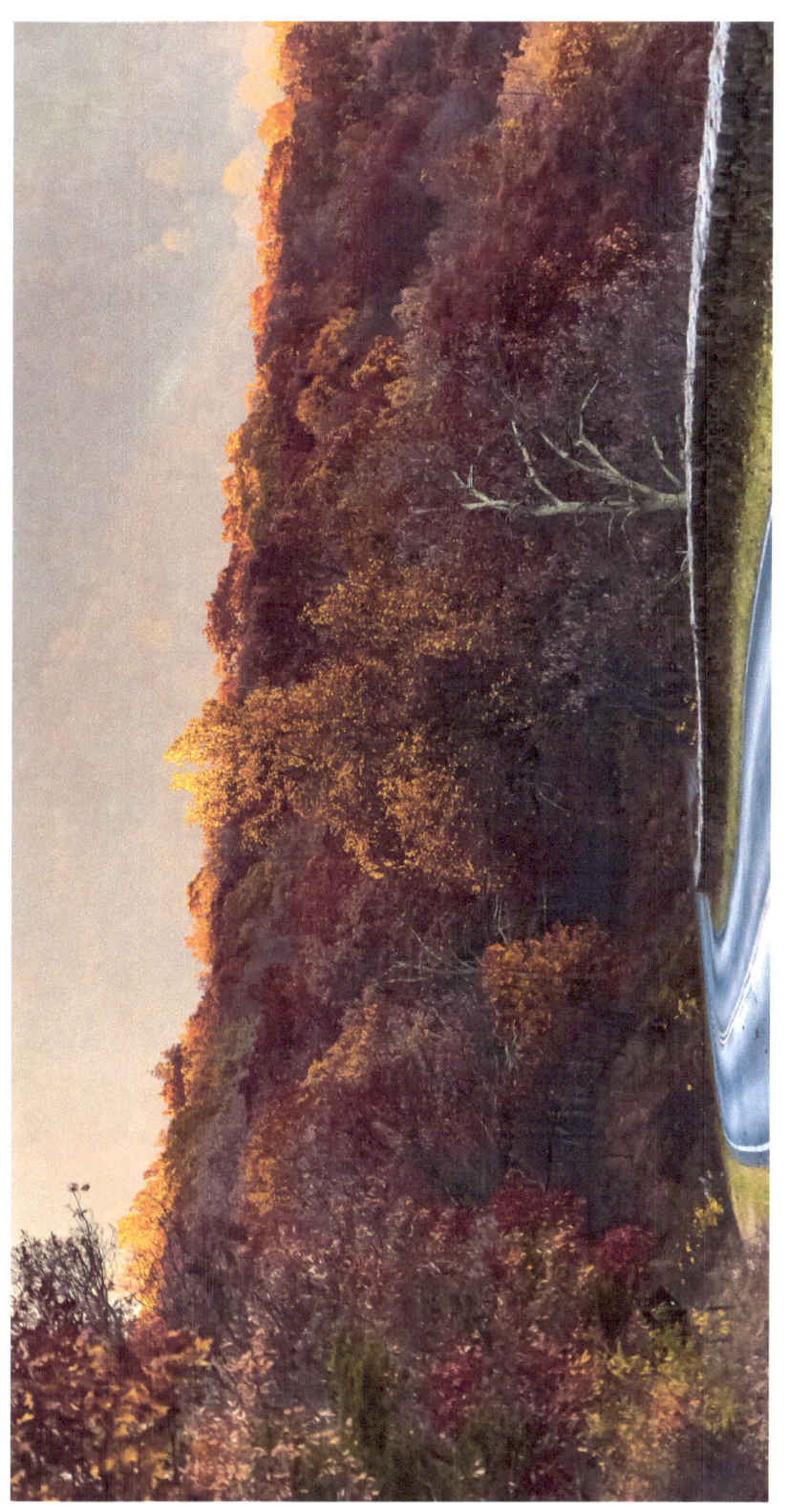

Shenandoah Valley Foliage - Gooney Run Overlook (2085 ft.)

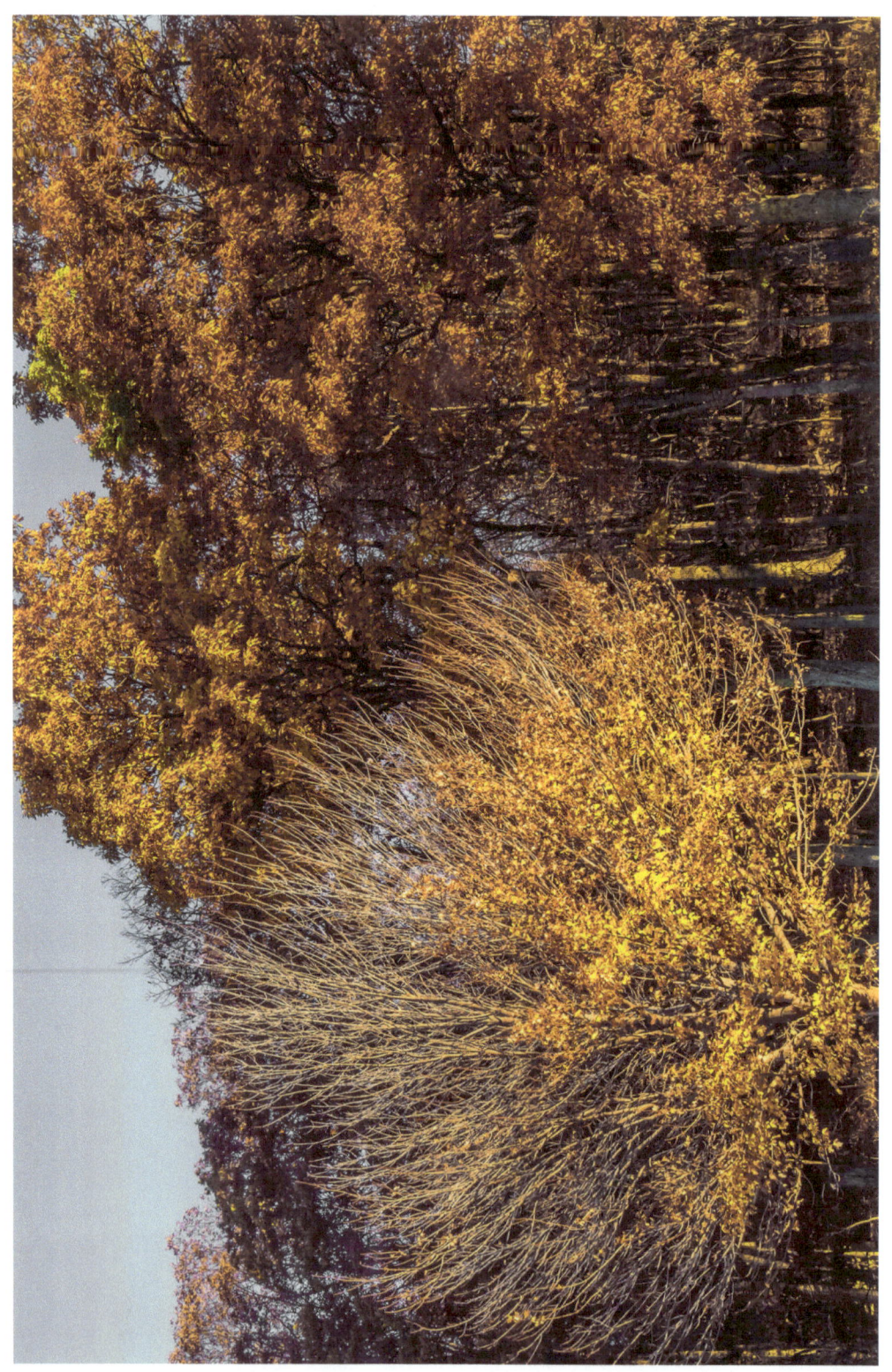

Yellow-Orange Fall Foliage - Gooney Manor Overlook (1920 ft.)

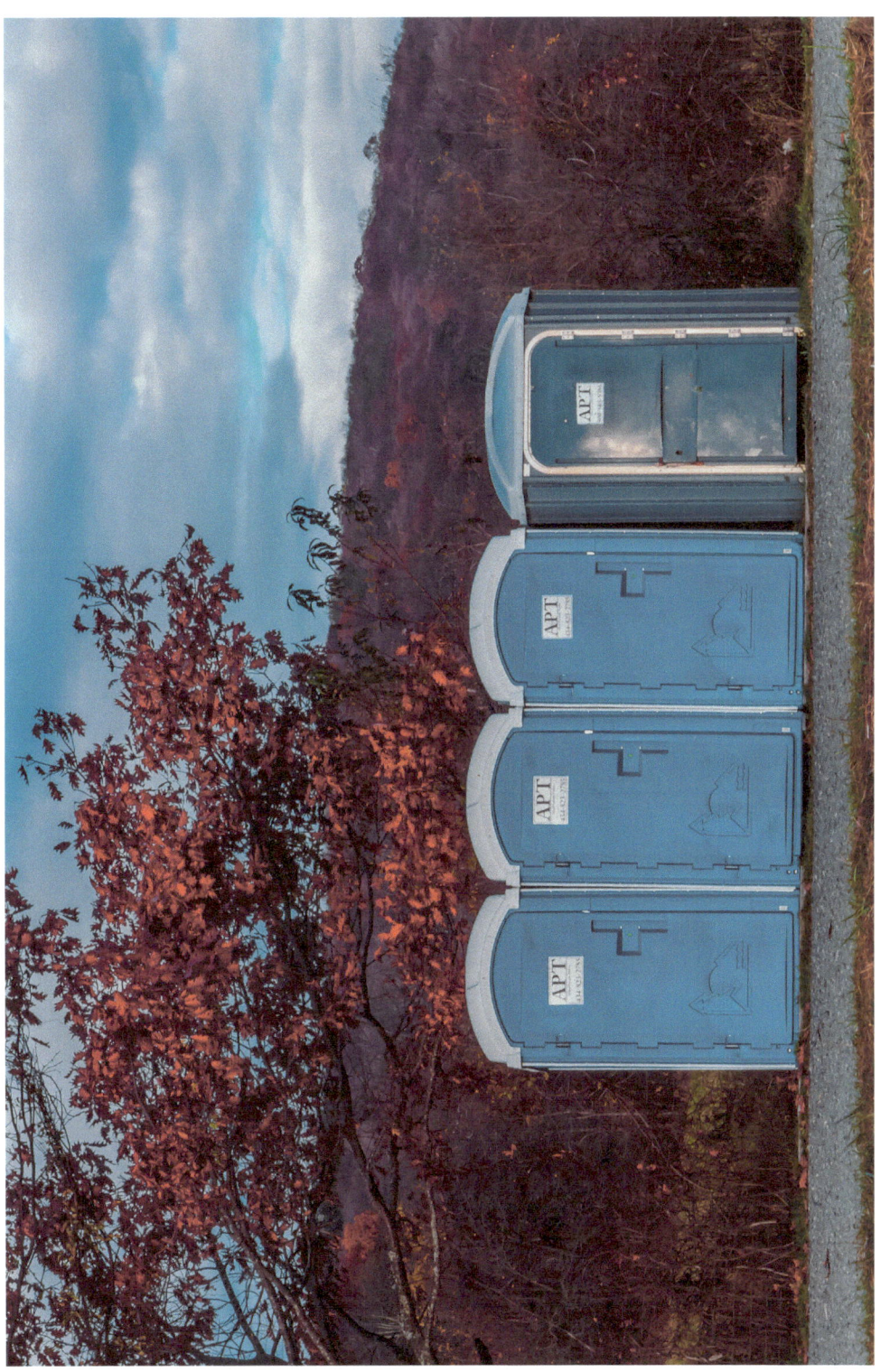

Restroom Accessibility at Beagle Gap - Calf Mountain Overlook (2485 ft.)

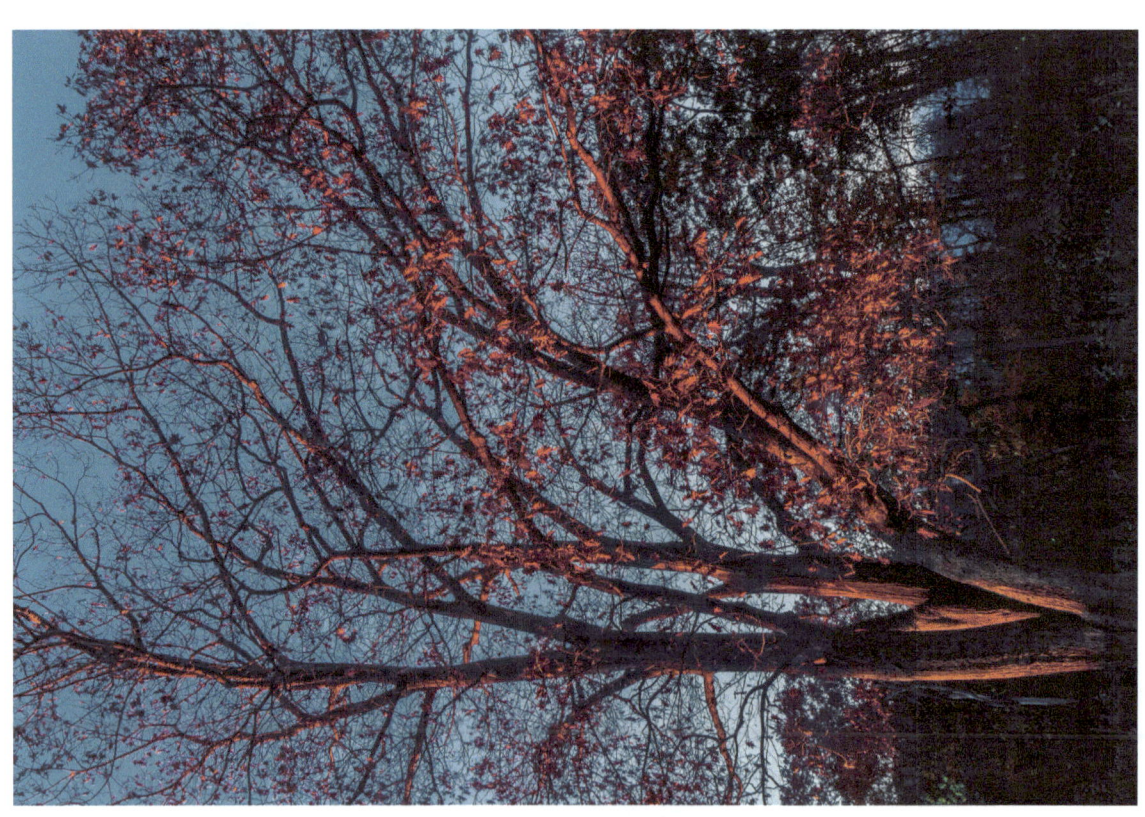

**Quality of Light Reflecting Complementary Colors
Shenandoah Valley Overlook (1390 ft.)**

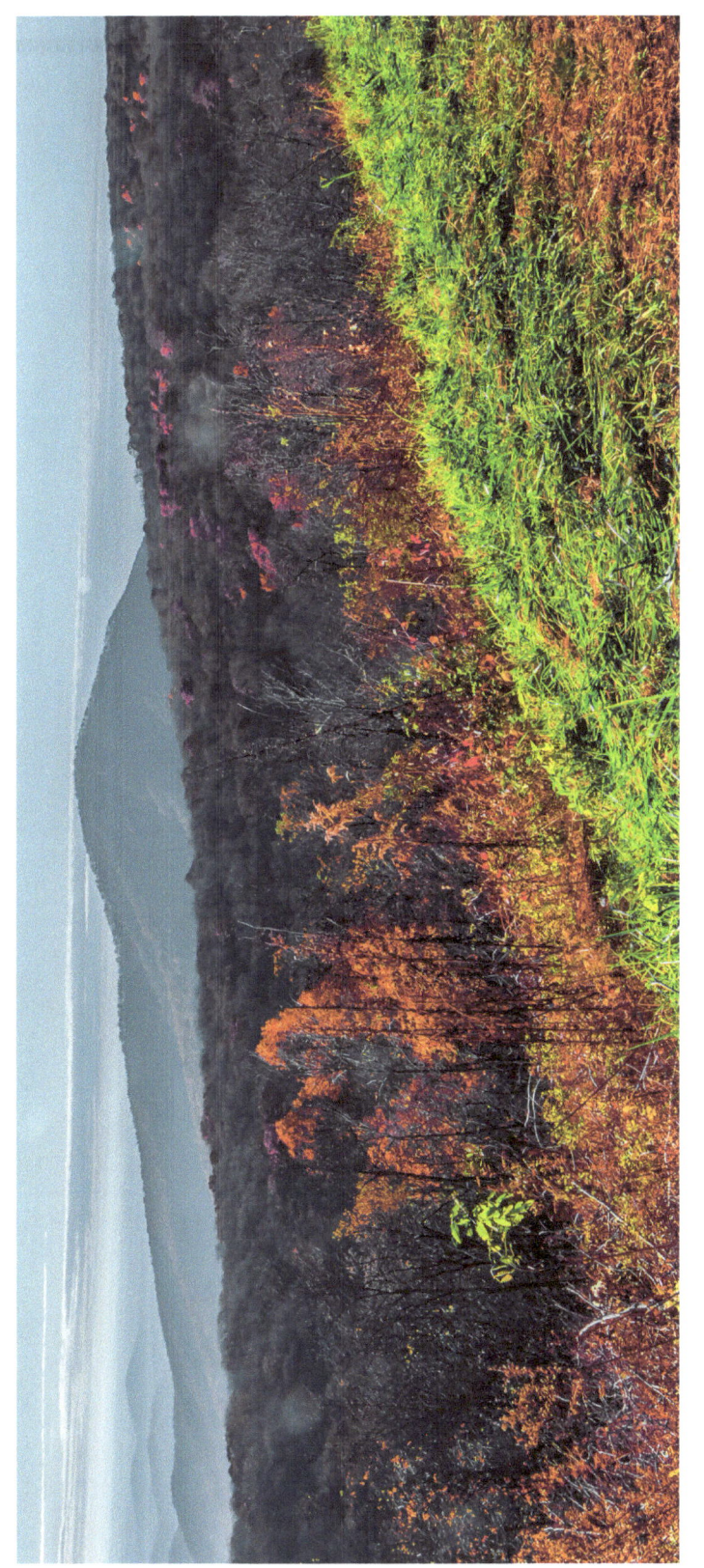

Natural Geometric Forms - Hogwallow Flats Overlook (2665 ft.)

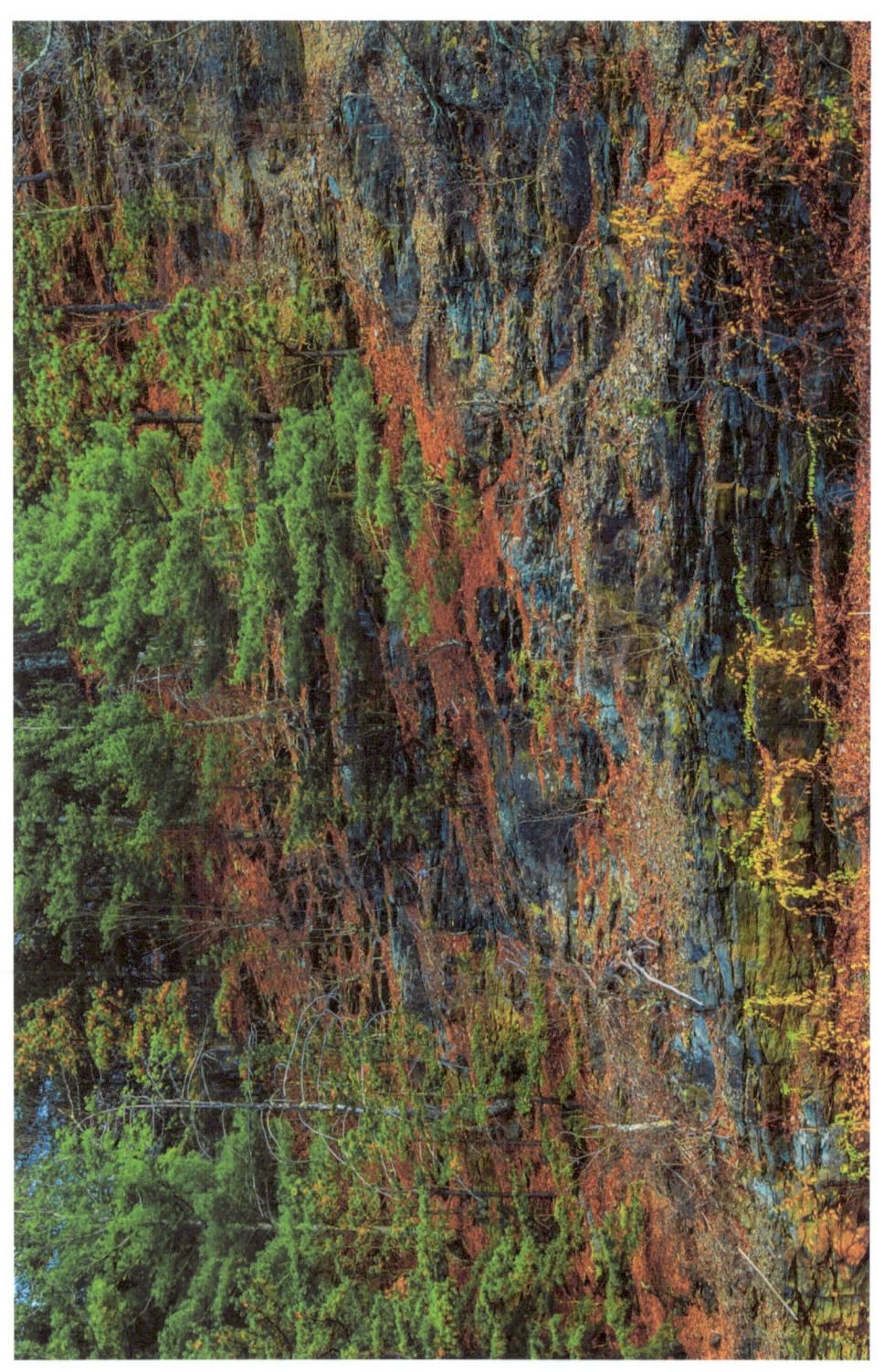

Rocky Pathways - Horsehead Overlook (2575 ft.)

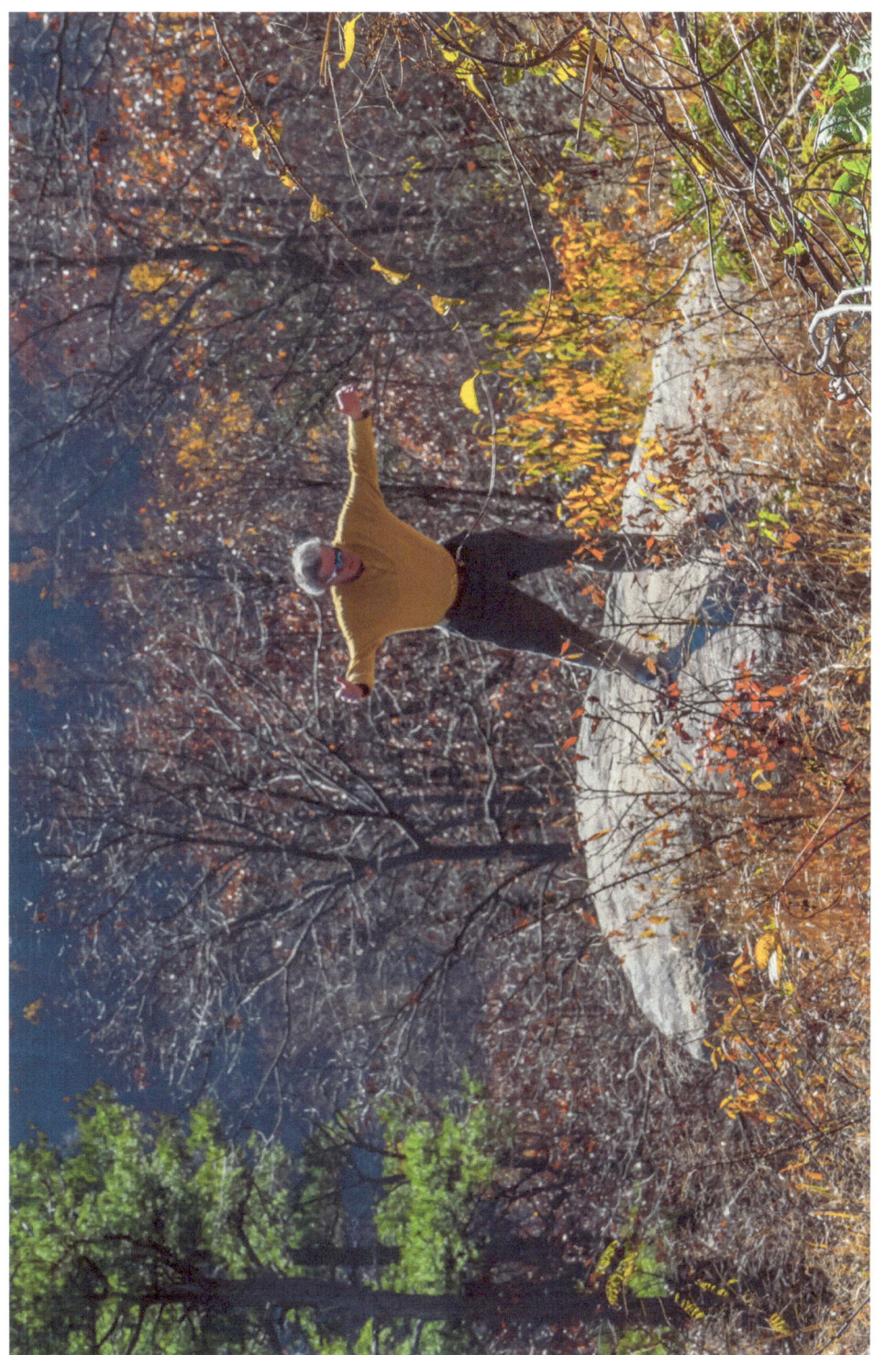

Brave Man on Rock - Hazel Mountain Overlook (2770 ft.)

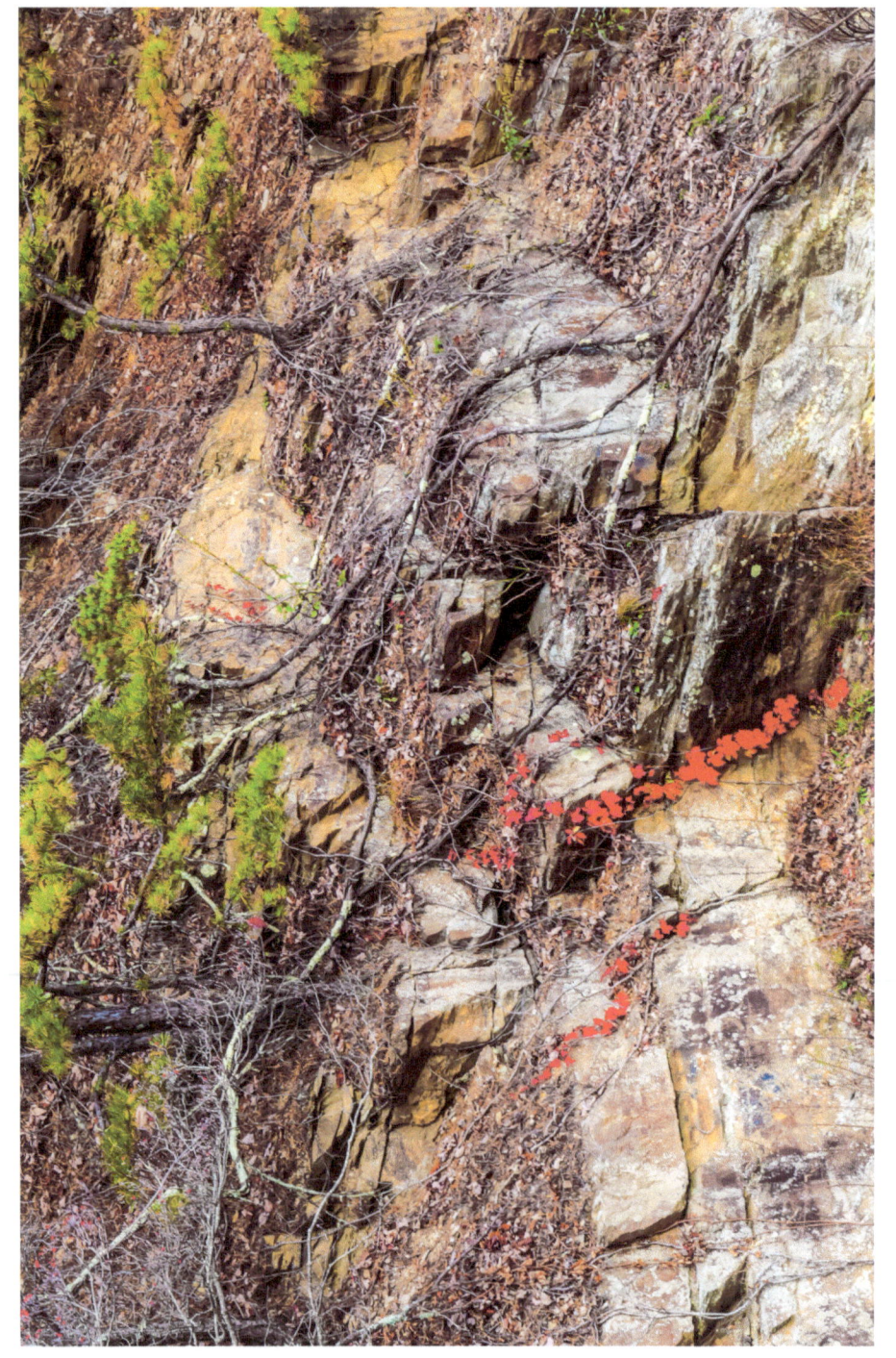

Scenic Vista - Sawmill Ridge Overlook (2210 ft.)

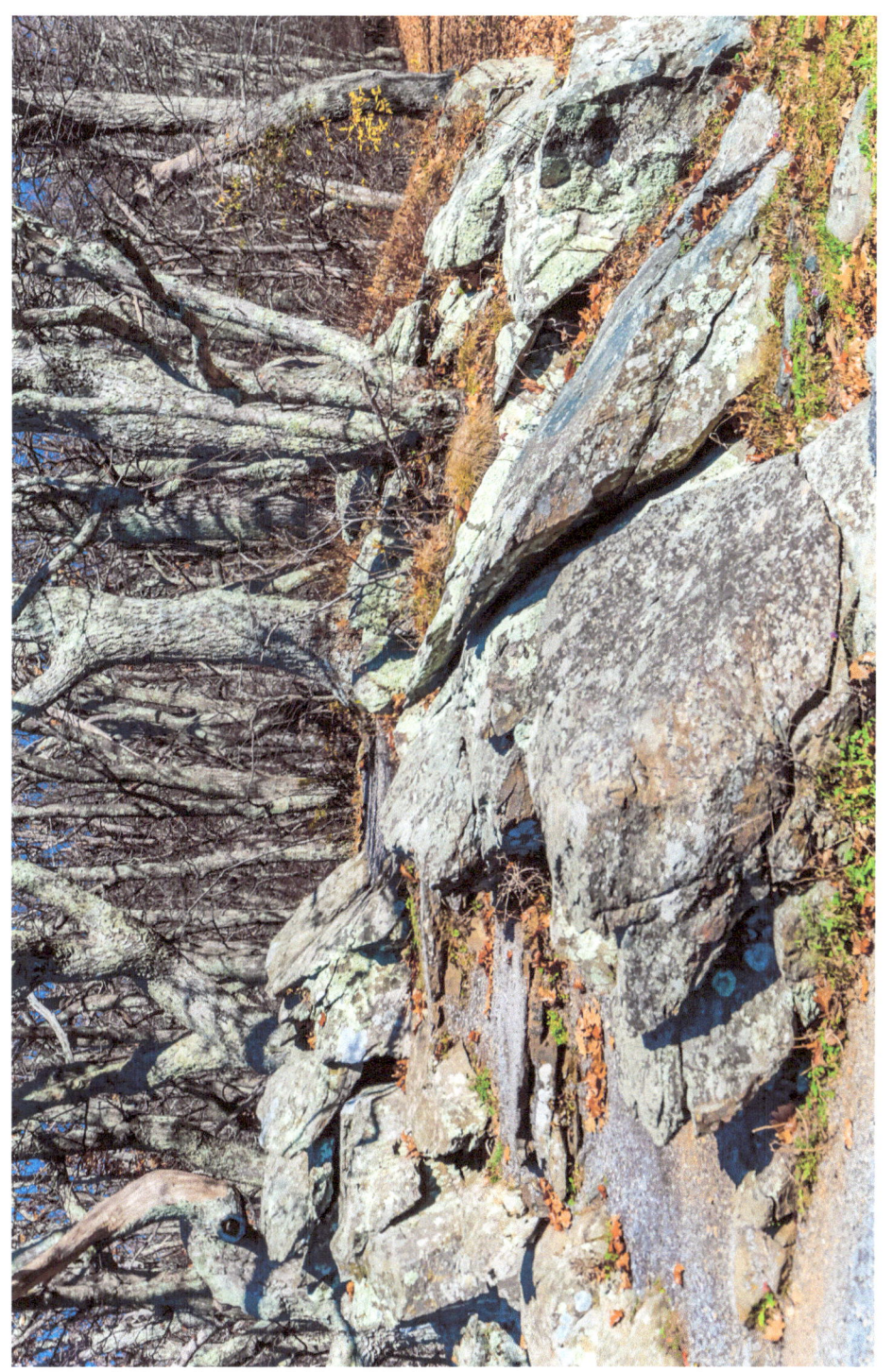

A Path Through a Rock Wall - Crescent Rock Overlook (3550 ft.)

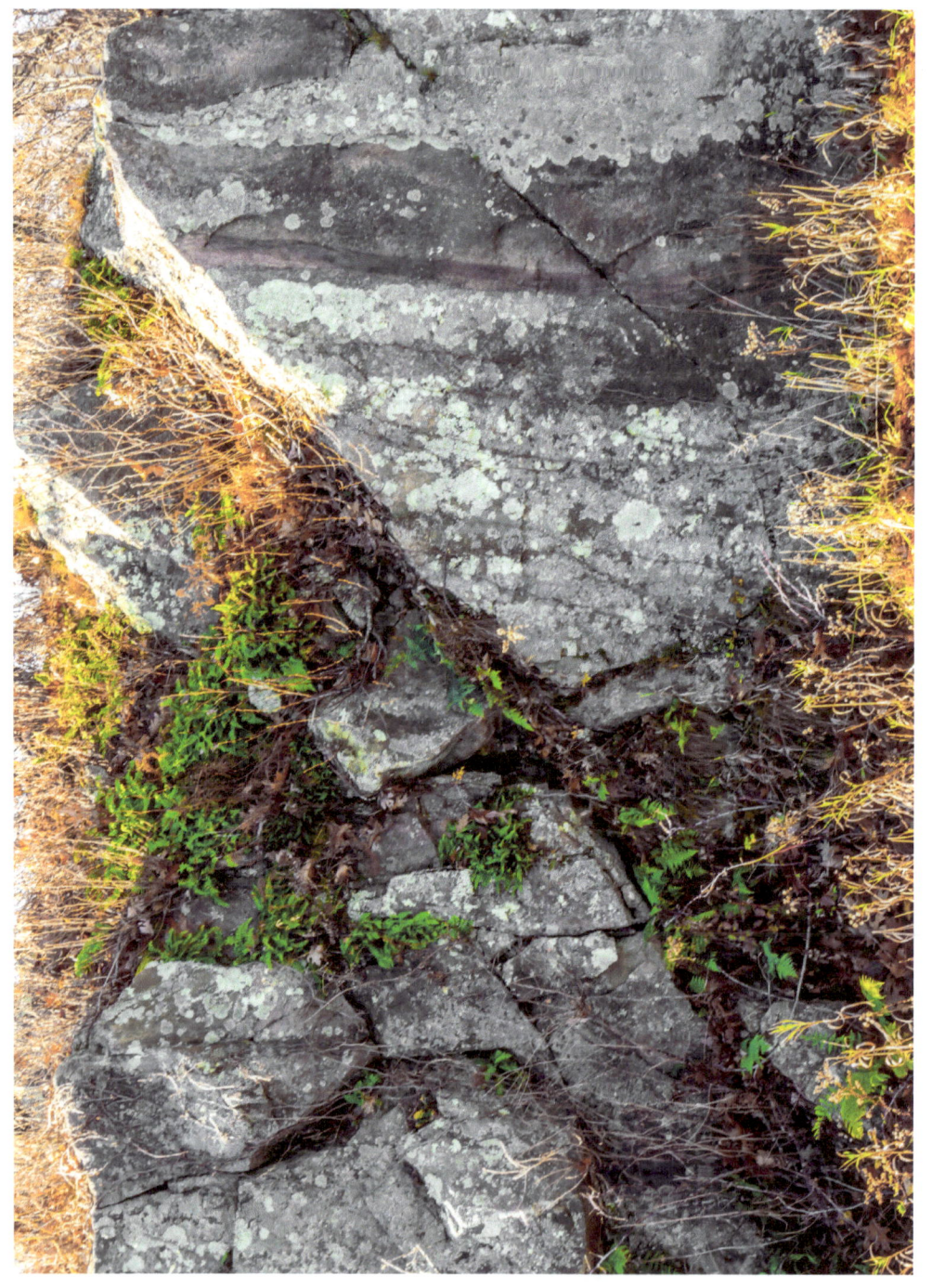

Rock Stone Texture on Rock Wall - Hogback Overlook (3385 ft.)

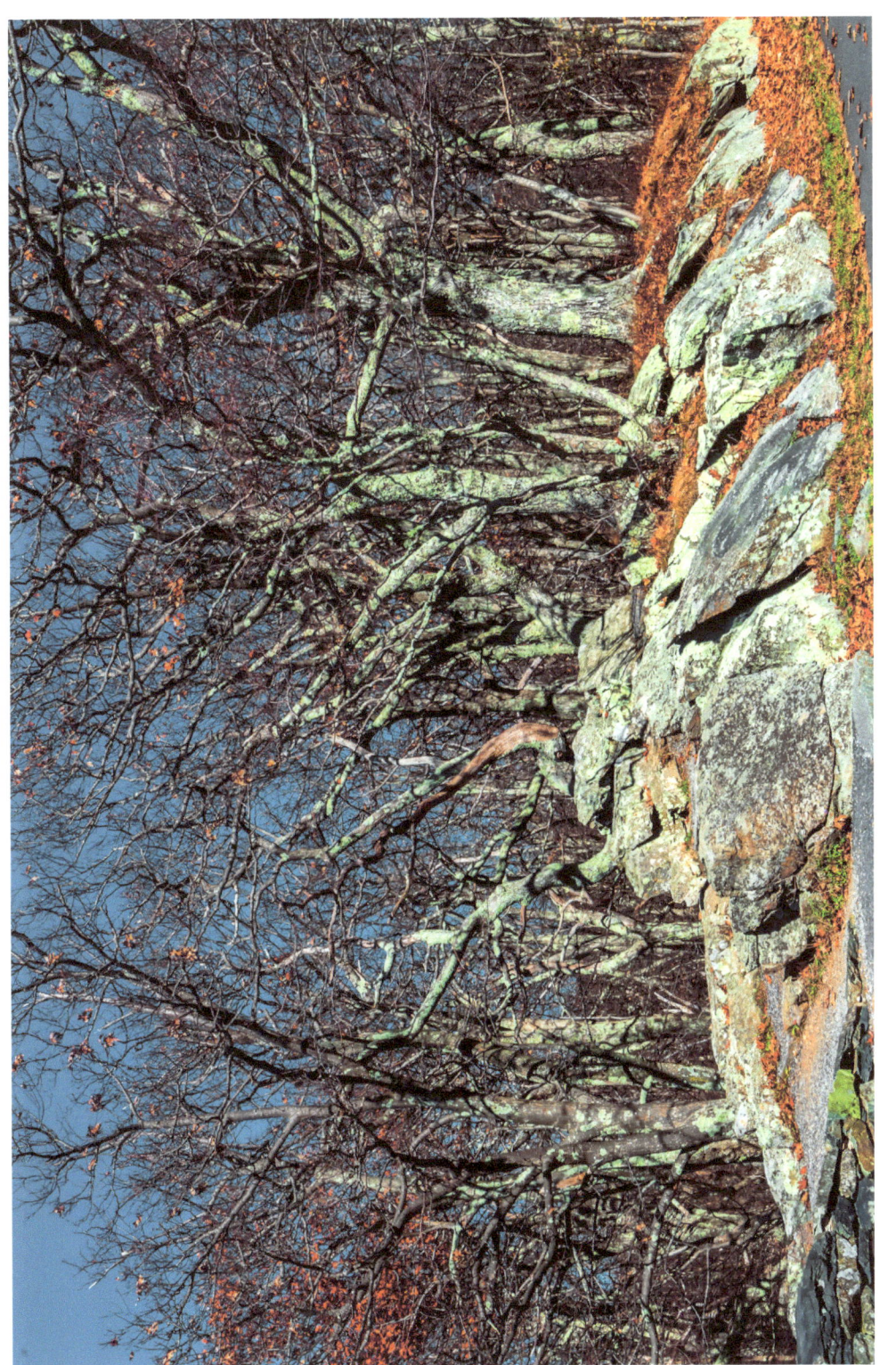

Rock and Tree Wall - Crescent Rock Overlook (3550 ft.)

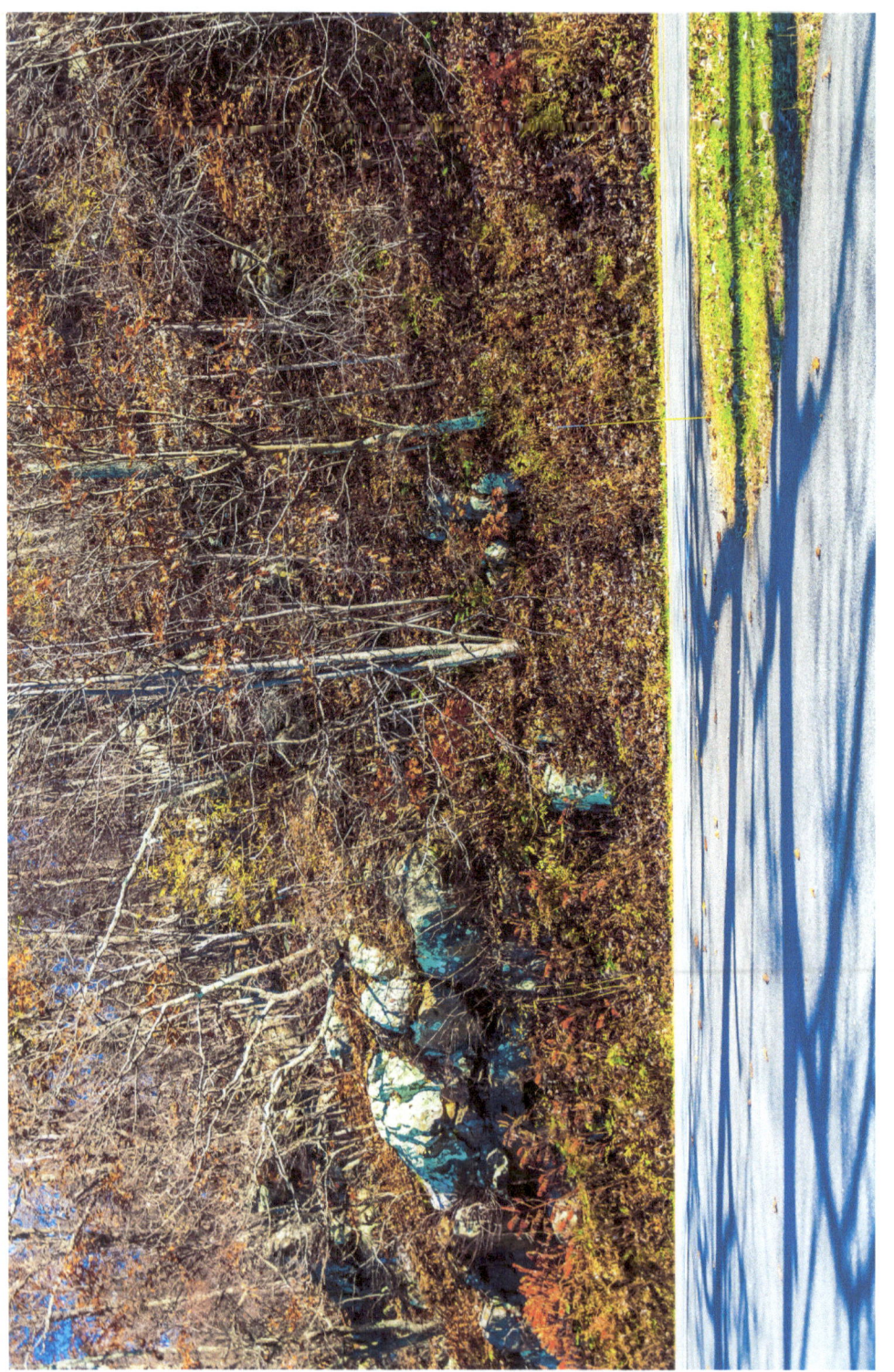

Tree Shadows on Rocks - Mount Marshall Overlook (2850 ft.)

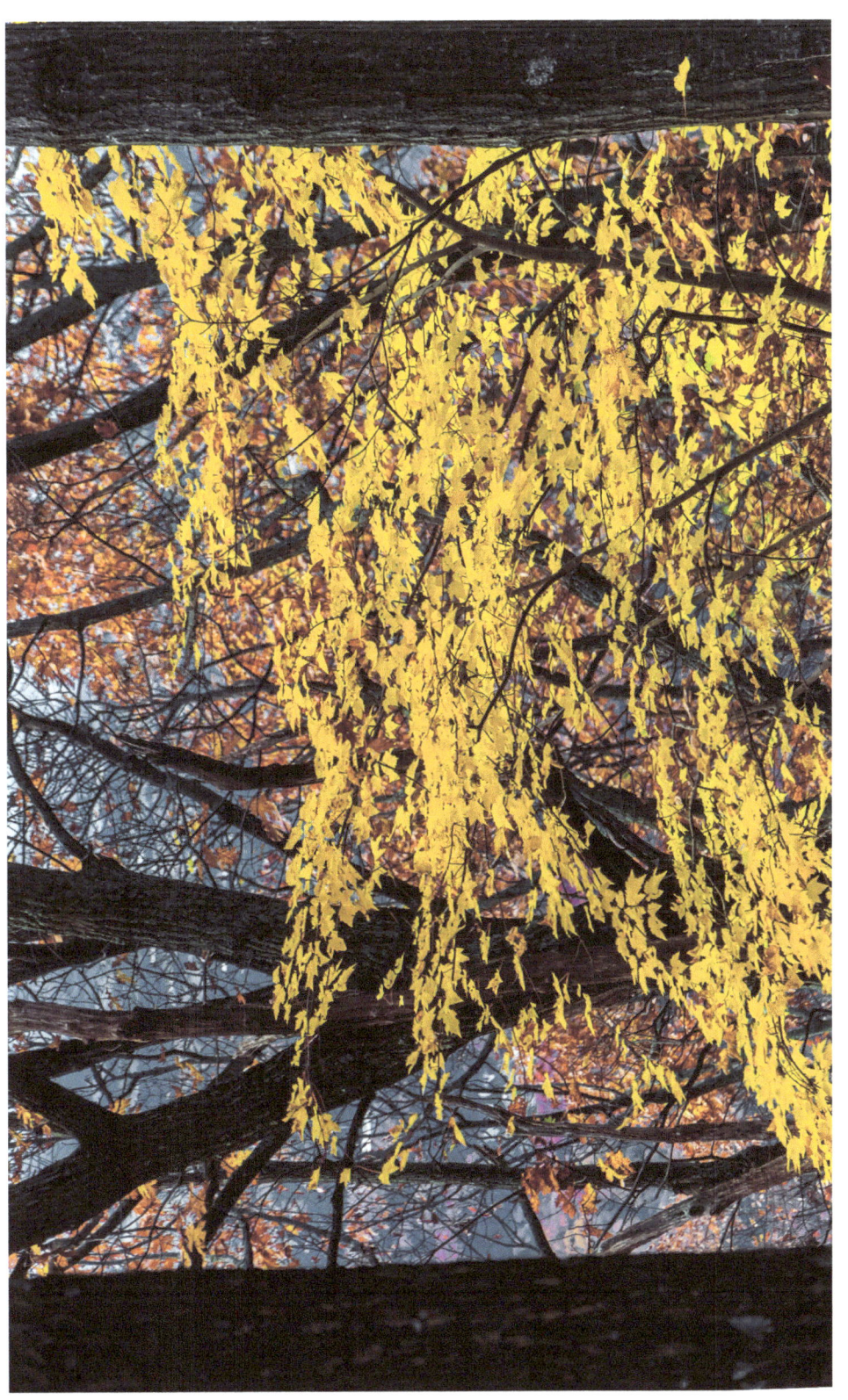

Tree Framed Mountain View - McCormick Gap Overlook (2455 ft.)

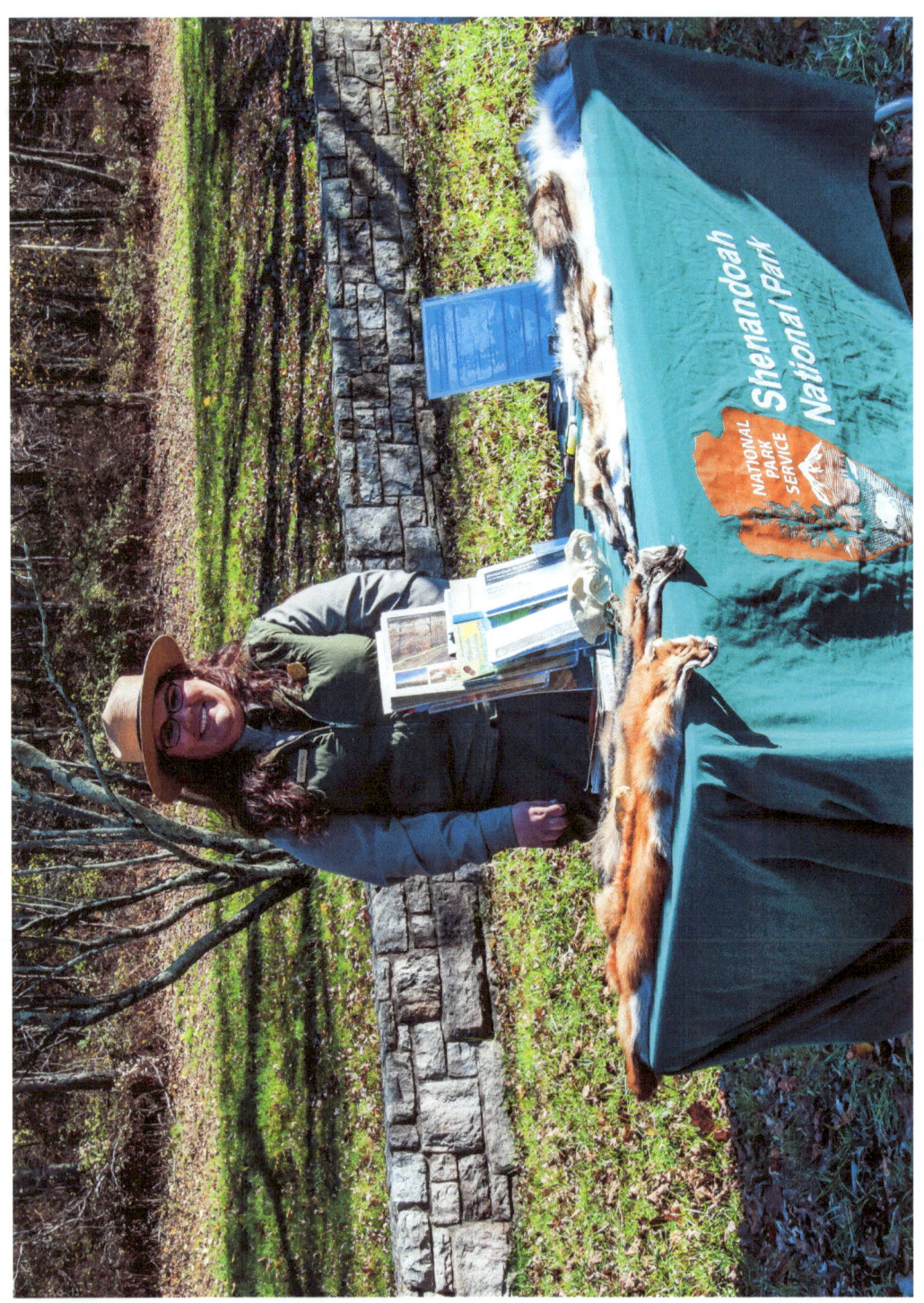

Ranger Display of Literature and Artifacts at Wayside Comfort Station

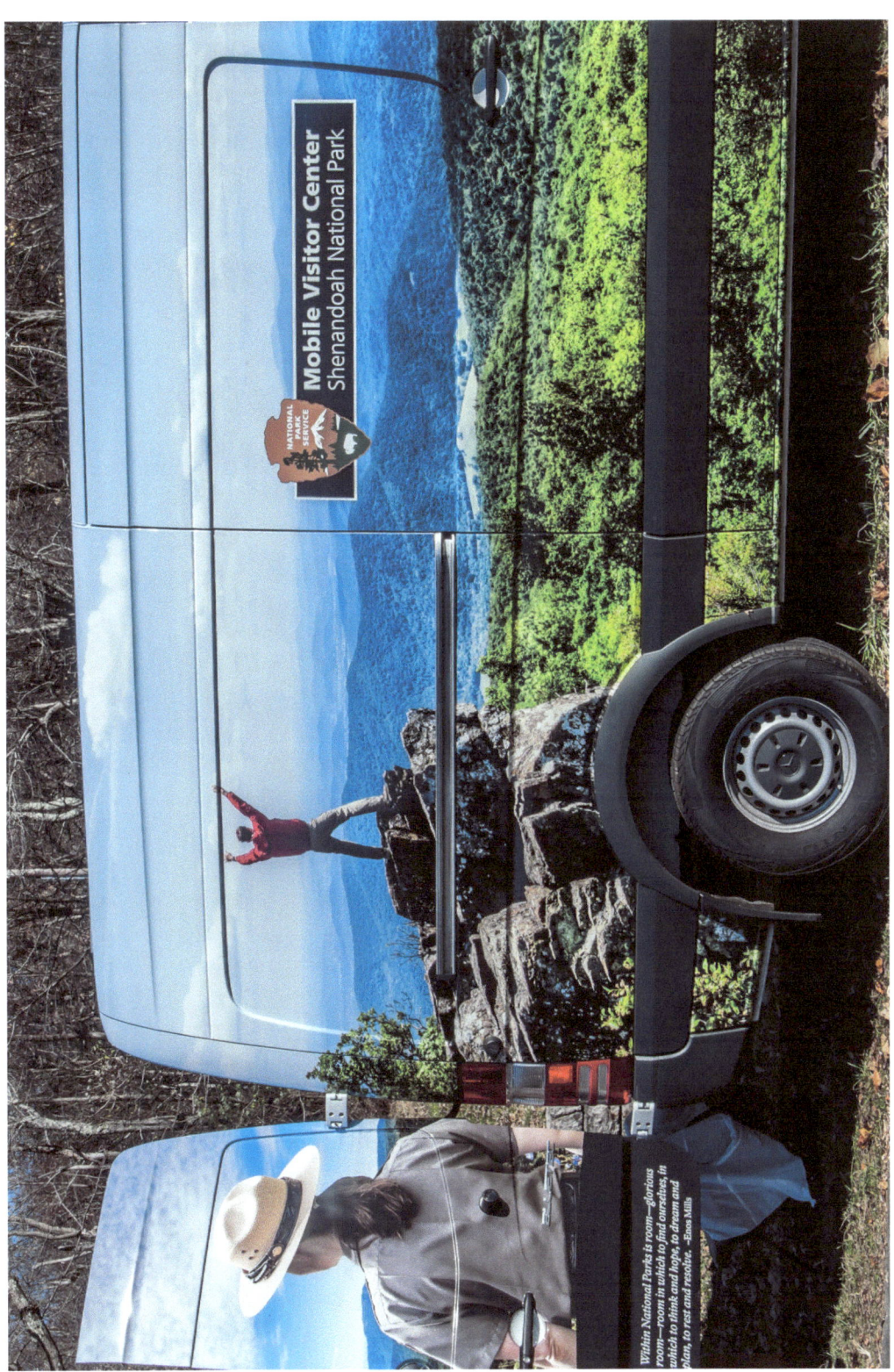

Mobile Visitor Center at Shenandoah National Park- Wayside Comfort Station

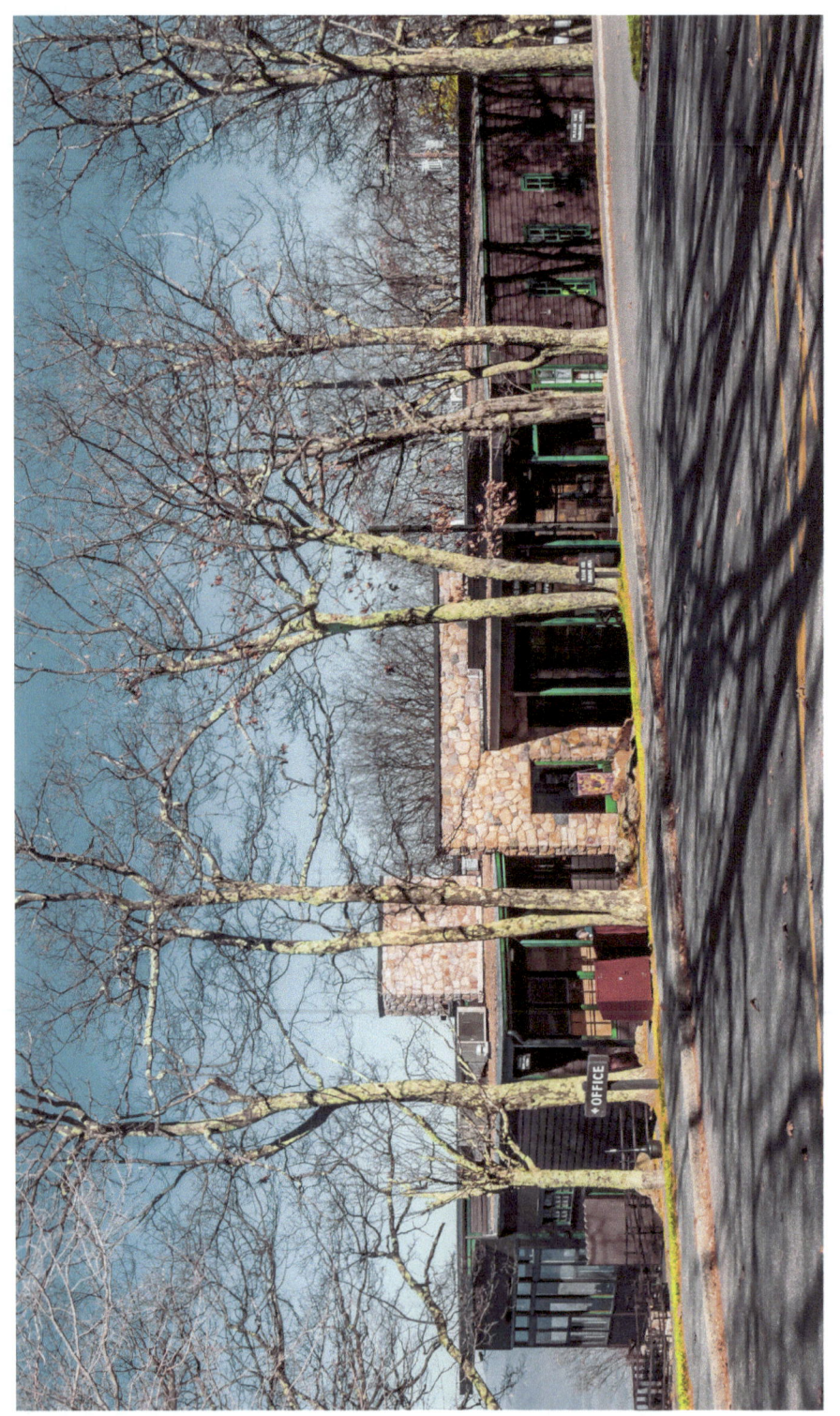

Skyland Resort in Luray, Virginia - The Highest Point of Elevation on Skyline Drive (3680 ft.)

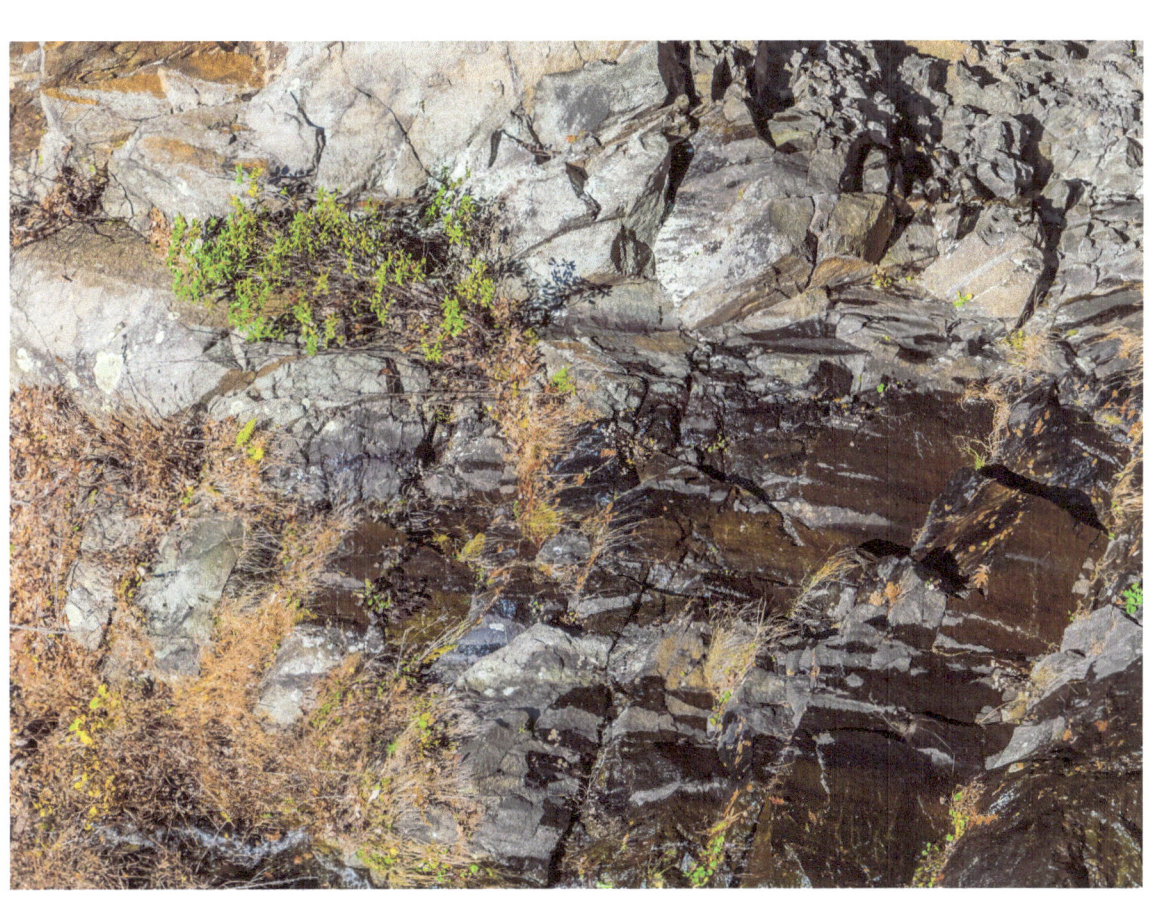

Mary's Rock Tunnel Side Wall - Tunnel Parking Overlook (2840 ft.)

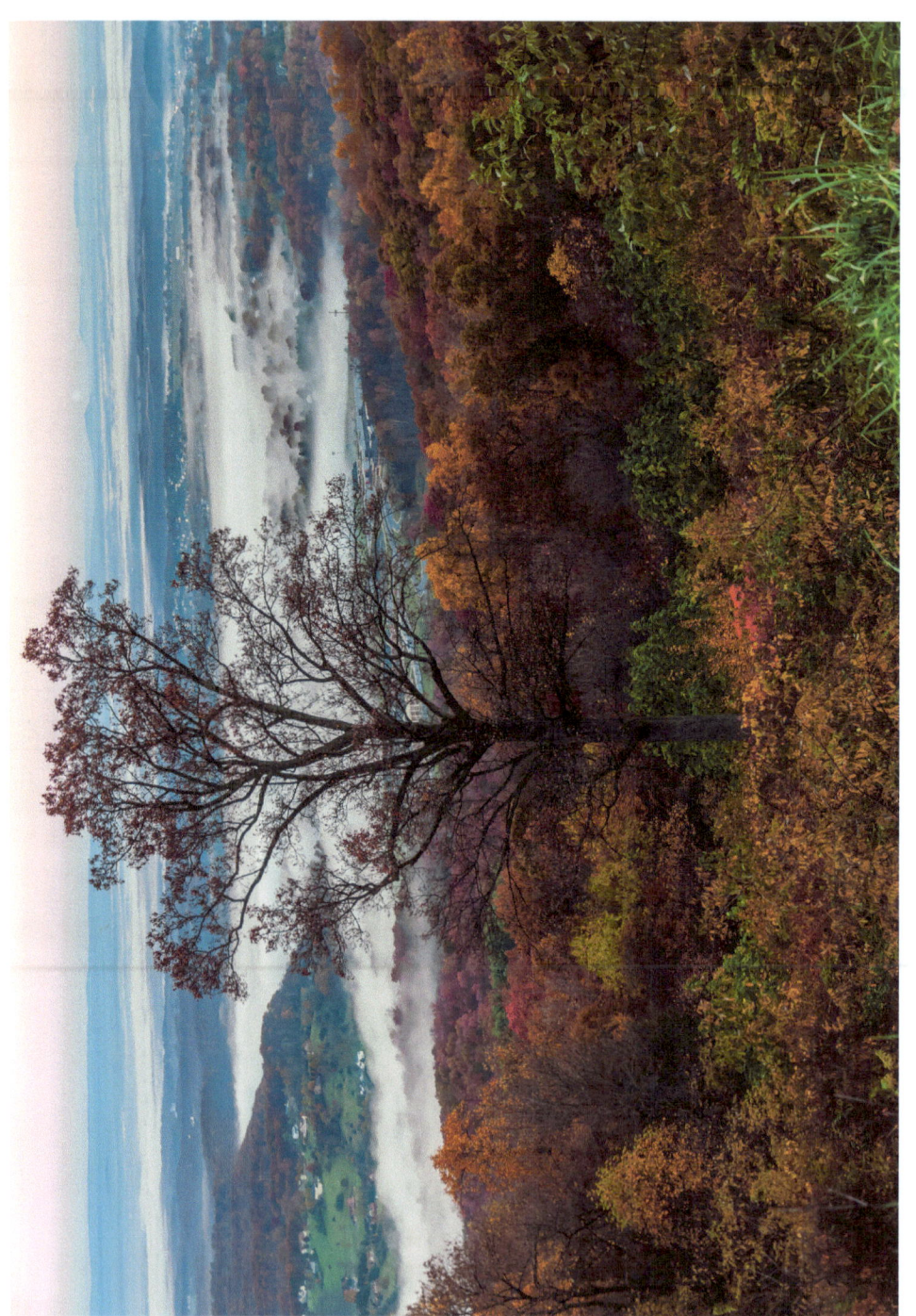

The Quintessential Look of Autumn - Thorofare Mountain Overlook (3595 ft.)

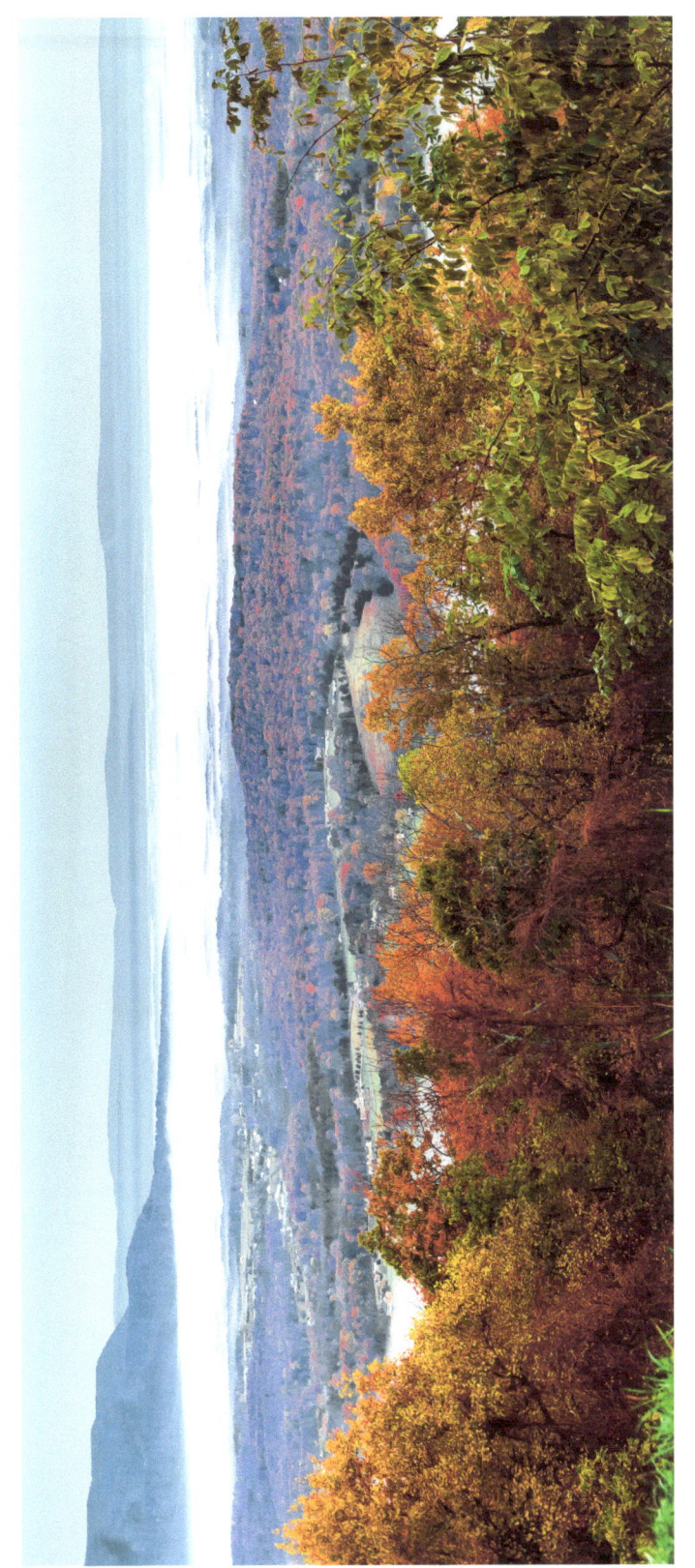

Skyline Drive Foliage View - Shenandoah Valley Overlook (1390 ft.)

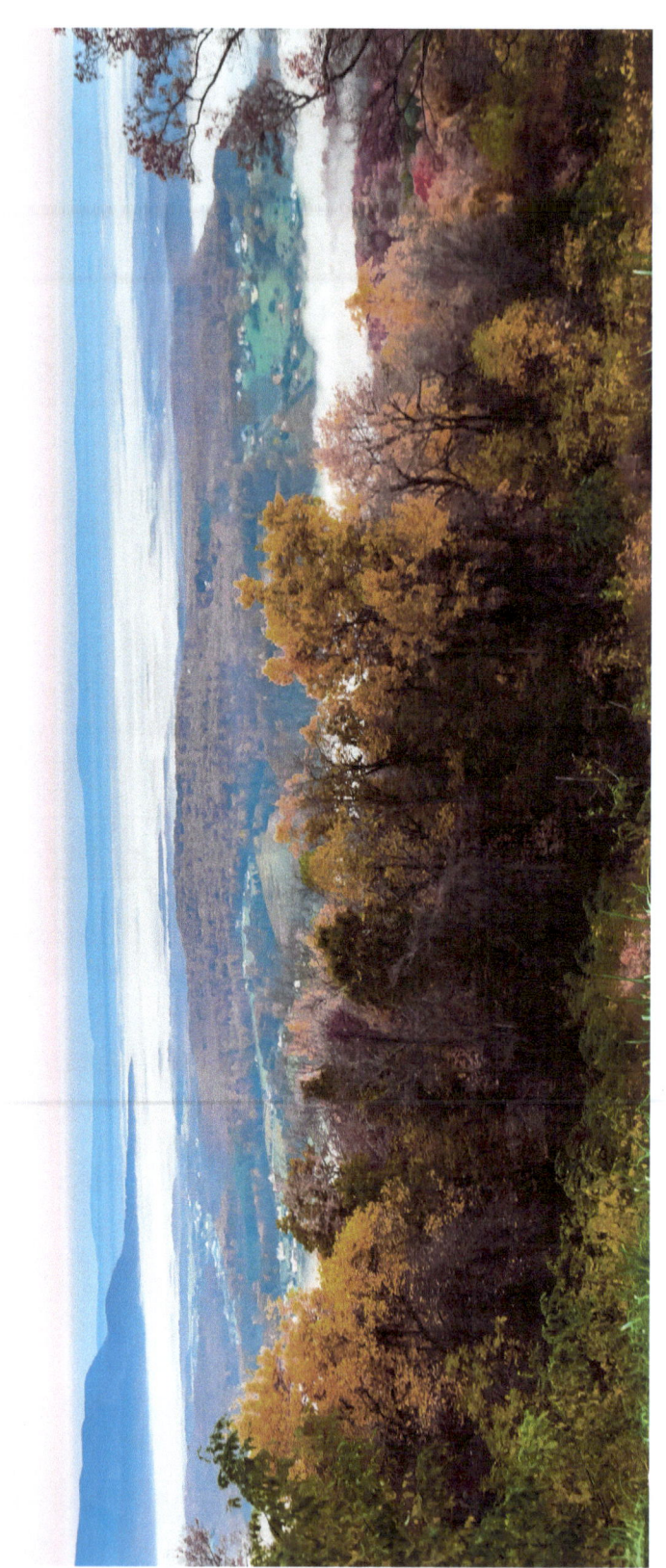

Landscape Autumn - Shenandoah Valley Overlook (1390 ft.)

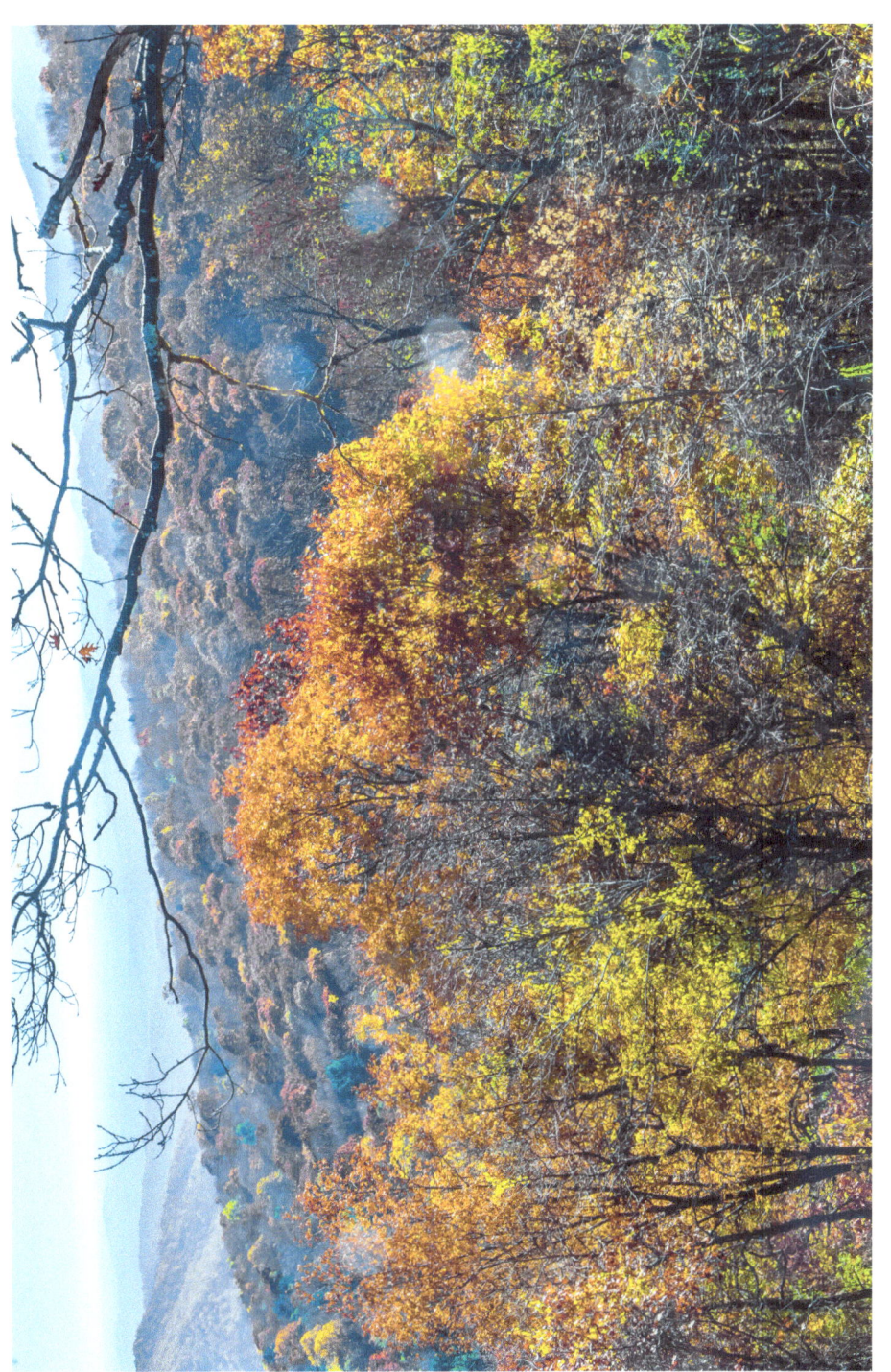

Colorful Tree Tops - Trayfoot Mountain Overlook (2575 ft.)

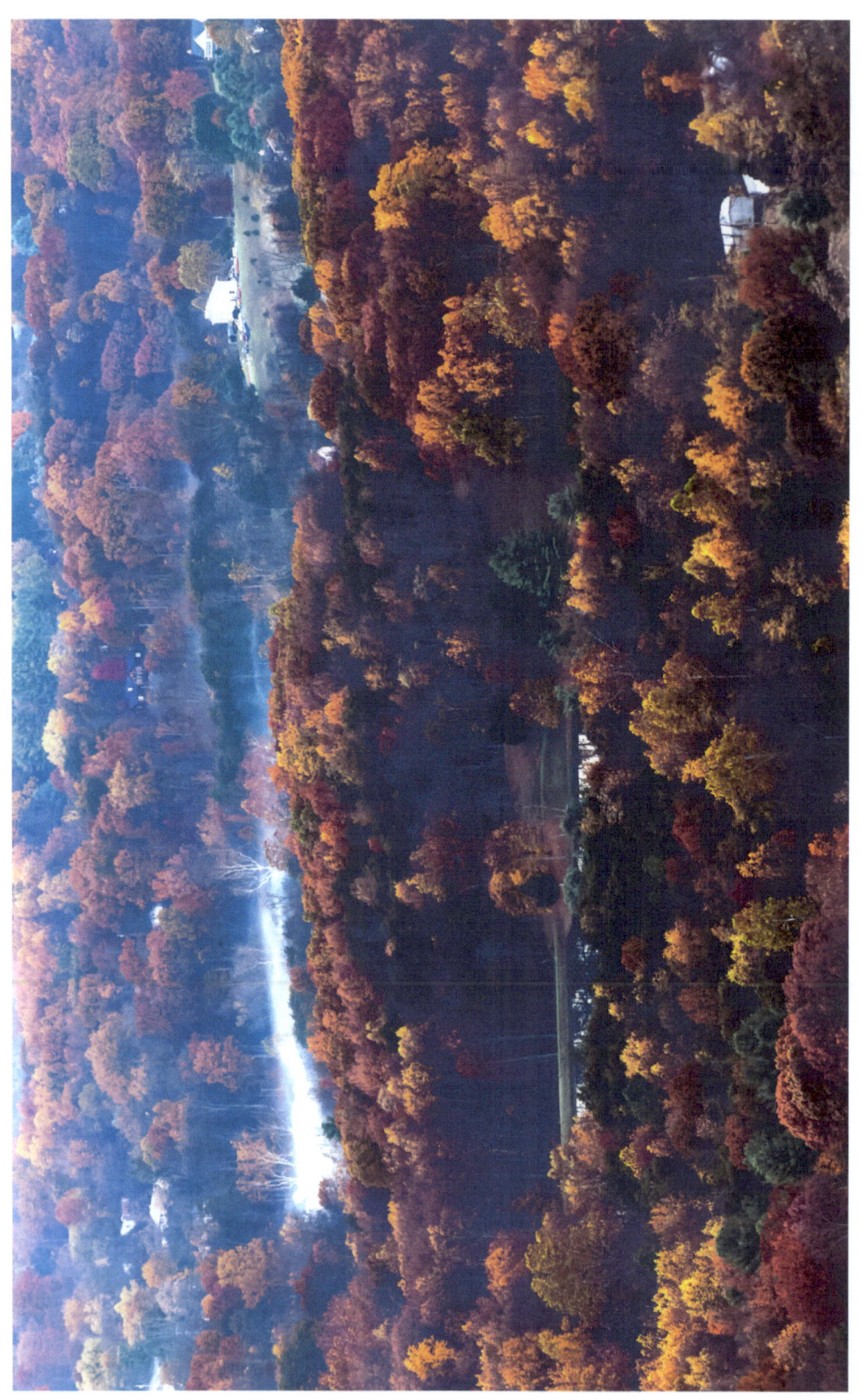

Foggy Mountain Scene - Shenandoah Valley Overlook (1390 ft.)

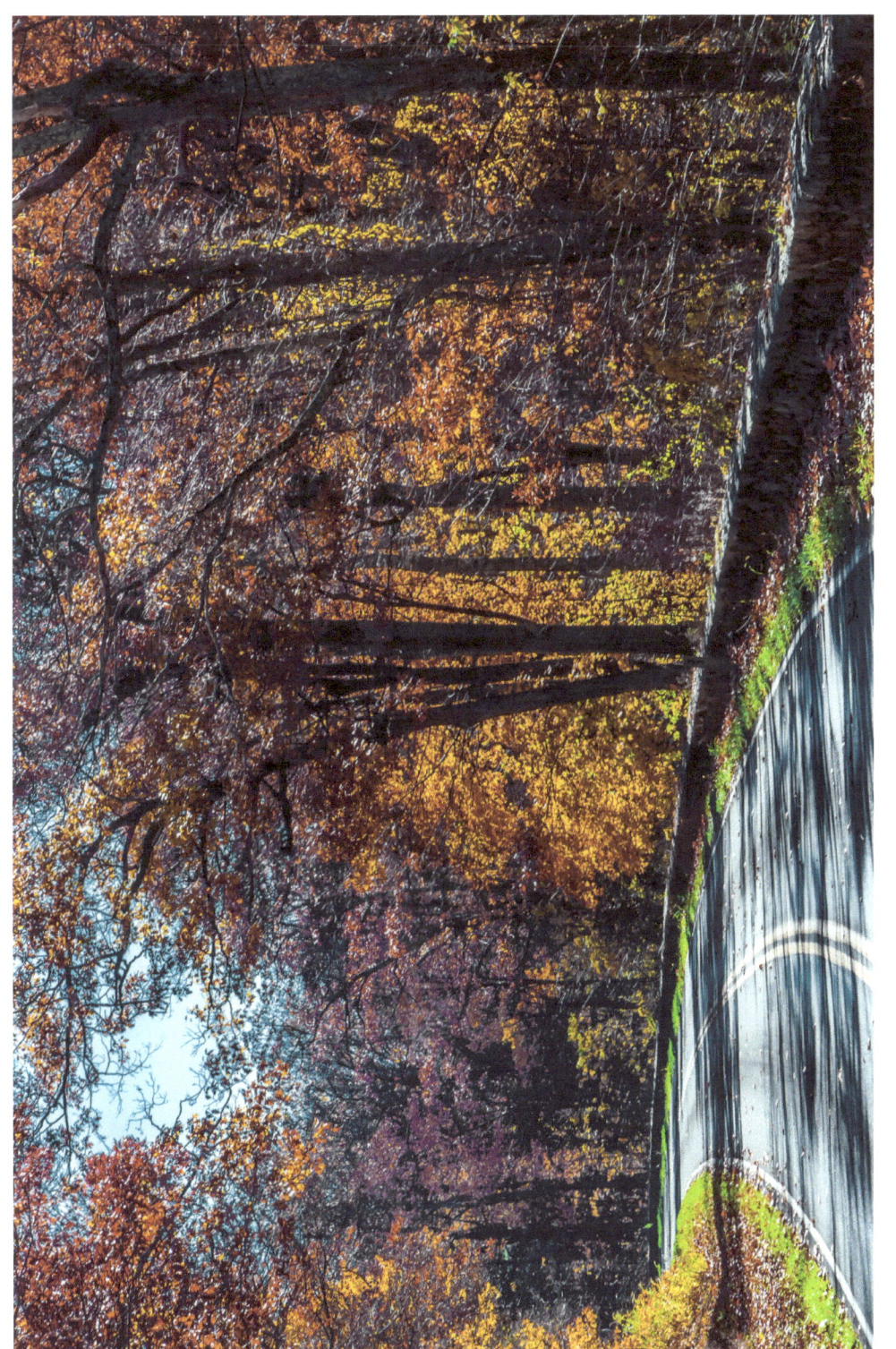

'Round the Mountain on Skyline Drive - Pass Mountain Overlook (2460 ft.)

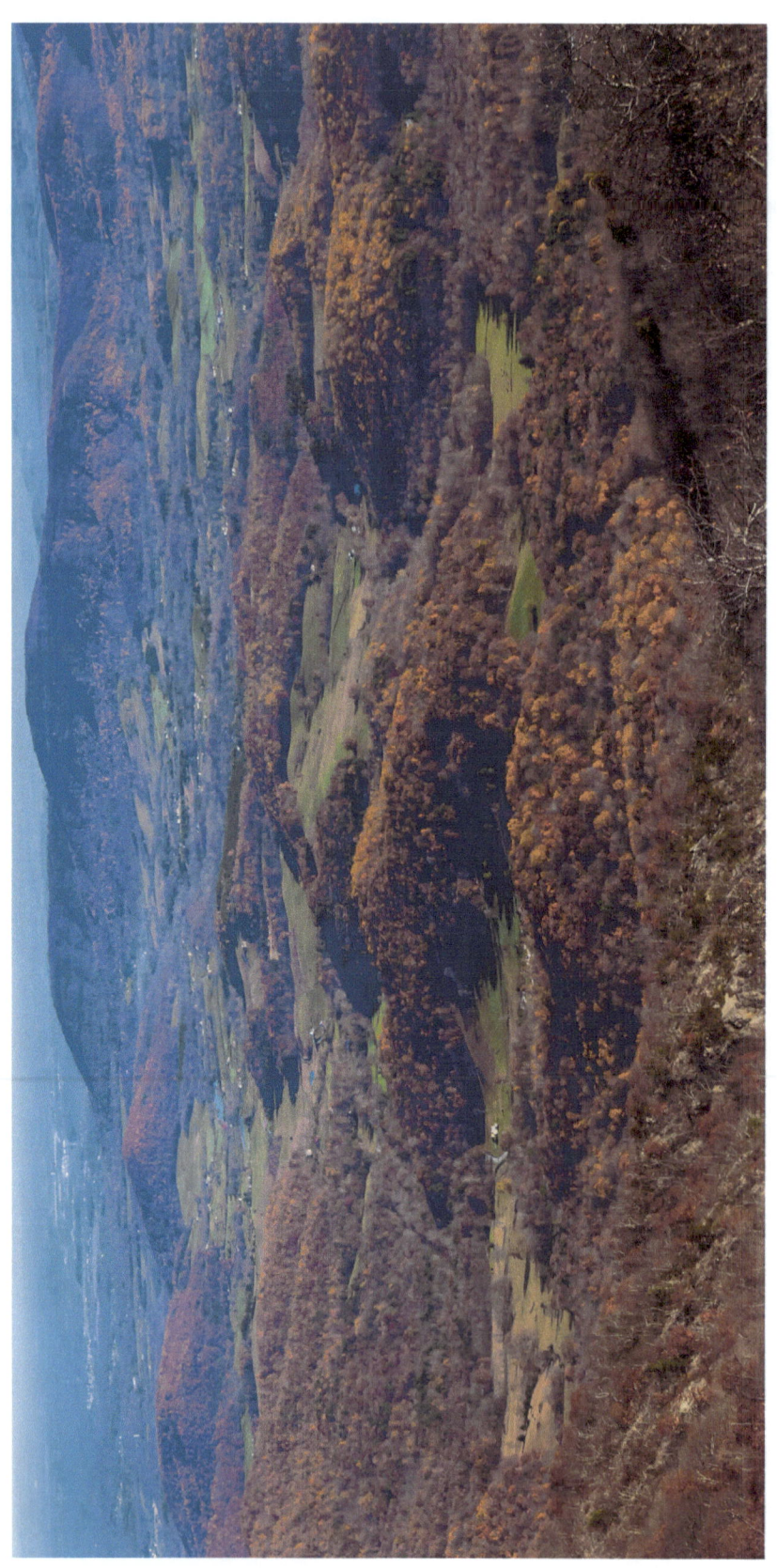

Spectacular Landscape View - Hogback Overlook (3385 ft.)

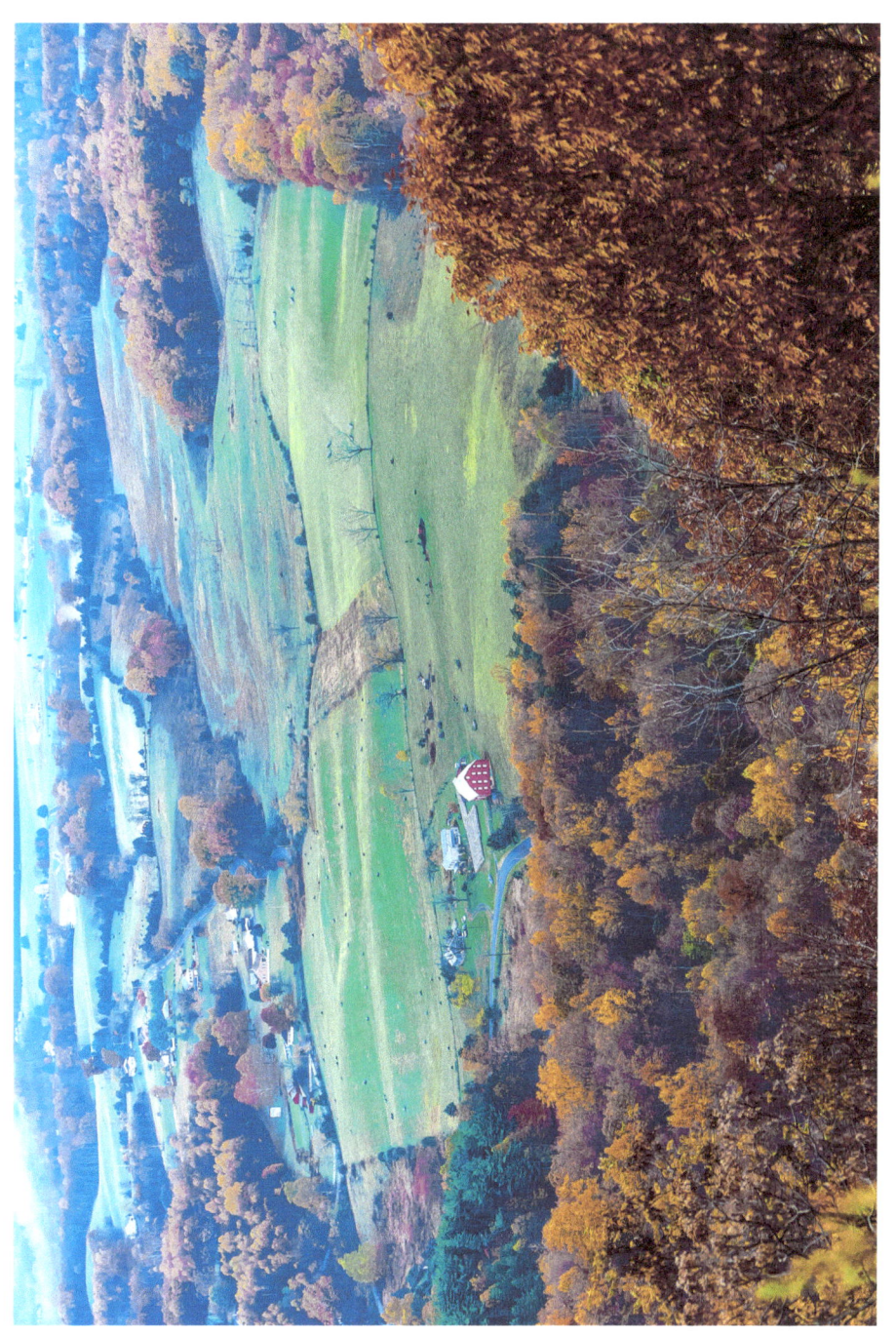

A Beautiful Shenandoah Landscape - Shenandoah Valley Overlook (1390 ft.)

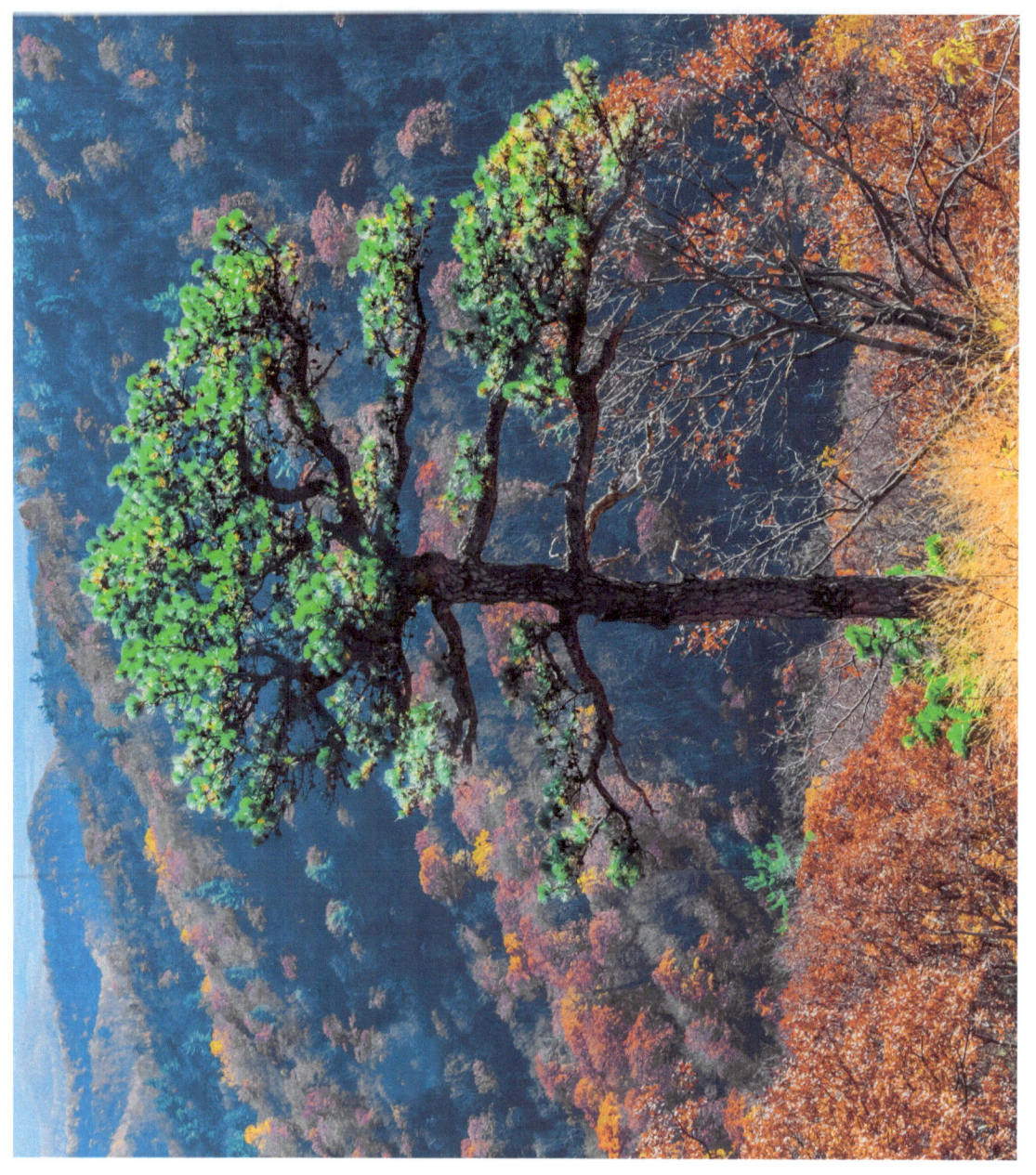

Green Mountain Tree on the Hazel Mountains - Hazel Mountain Overlook (2770 ft.)

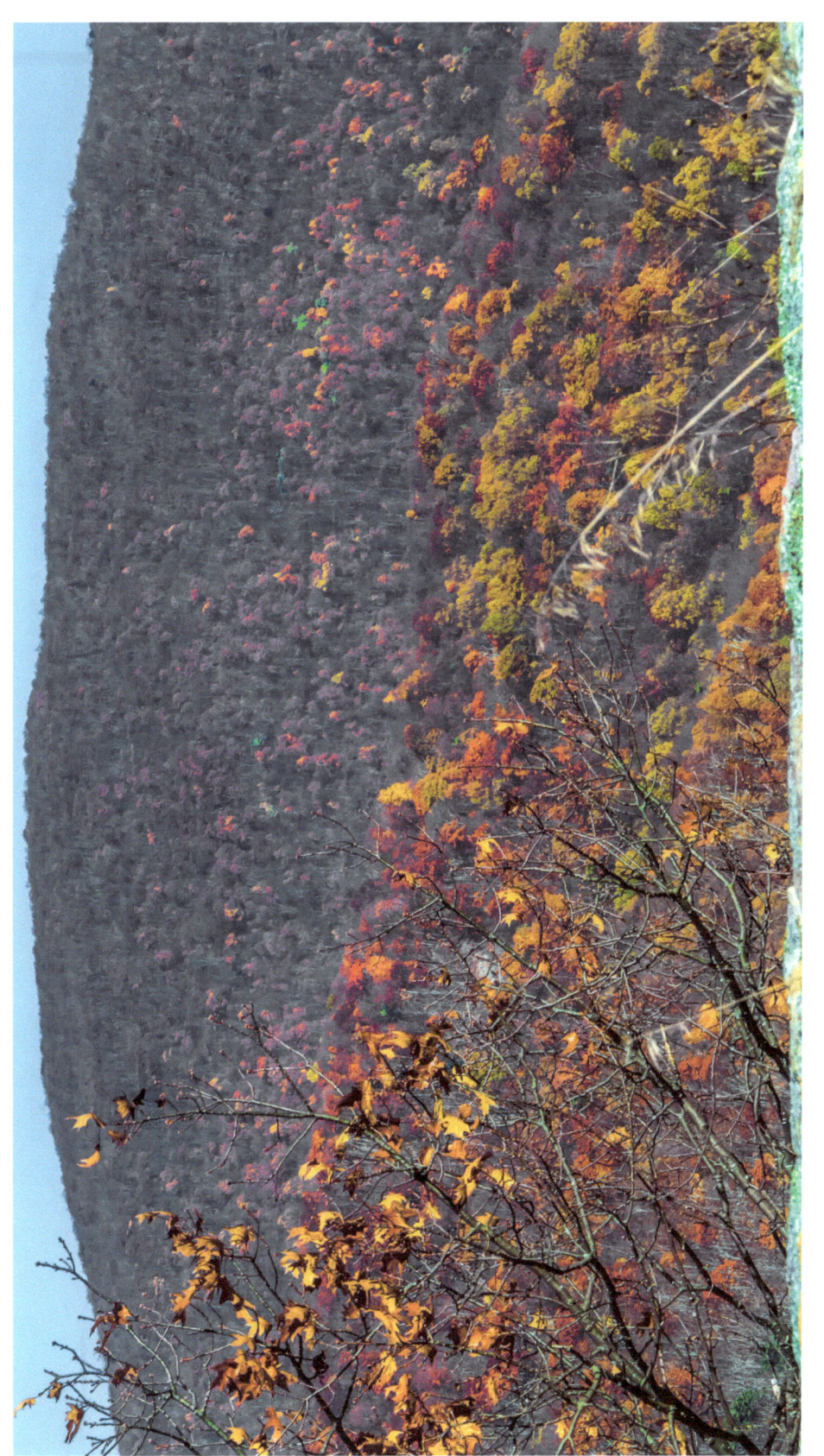

Blowing Mountain Leaves - Mount Marshall Overlook (2850 ft.)

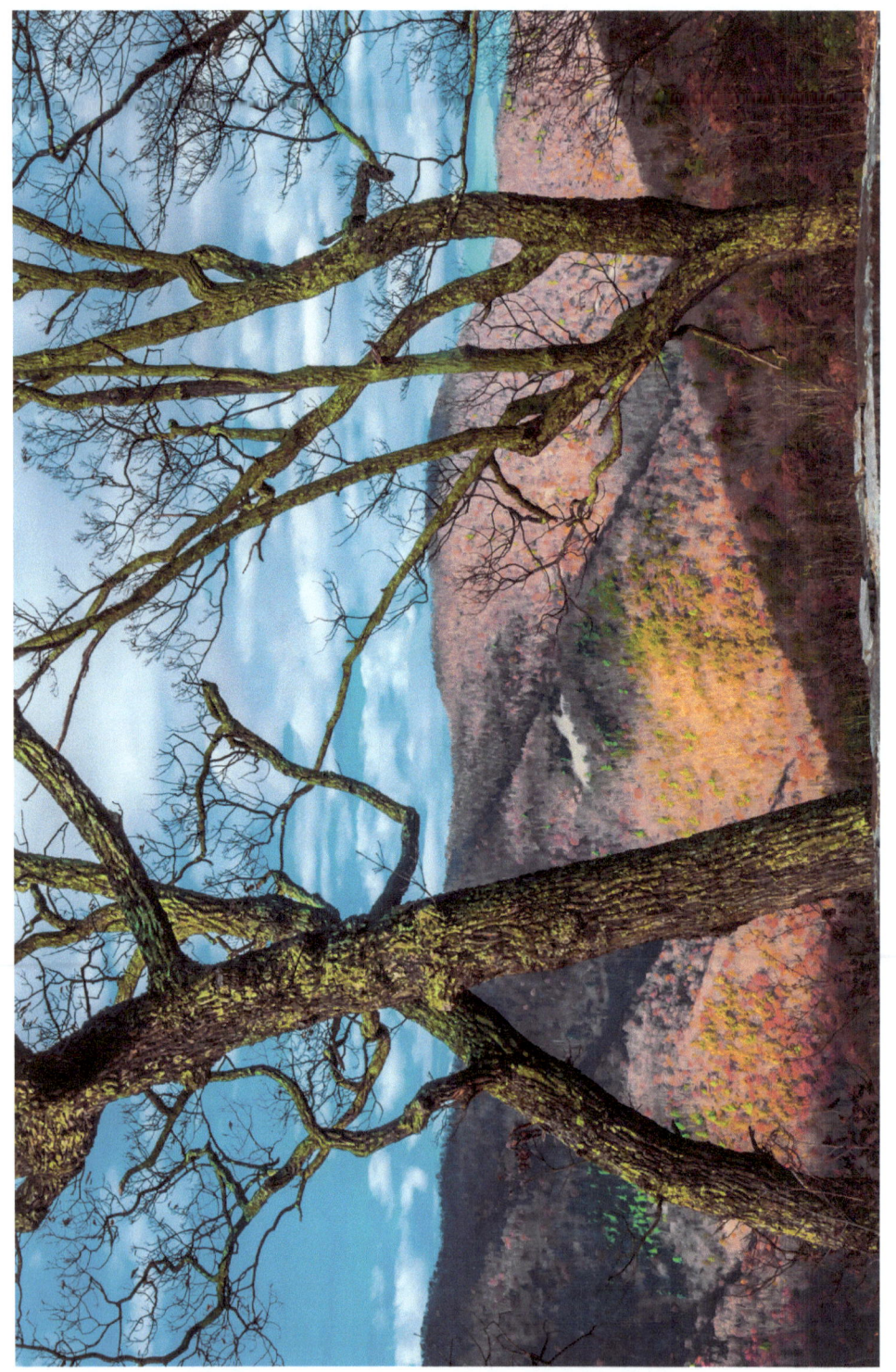

Leafless Trees and Vector Mountain - Horsehead Overlook (2575 ft.)

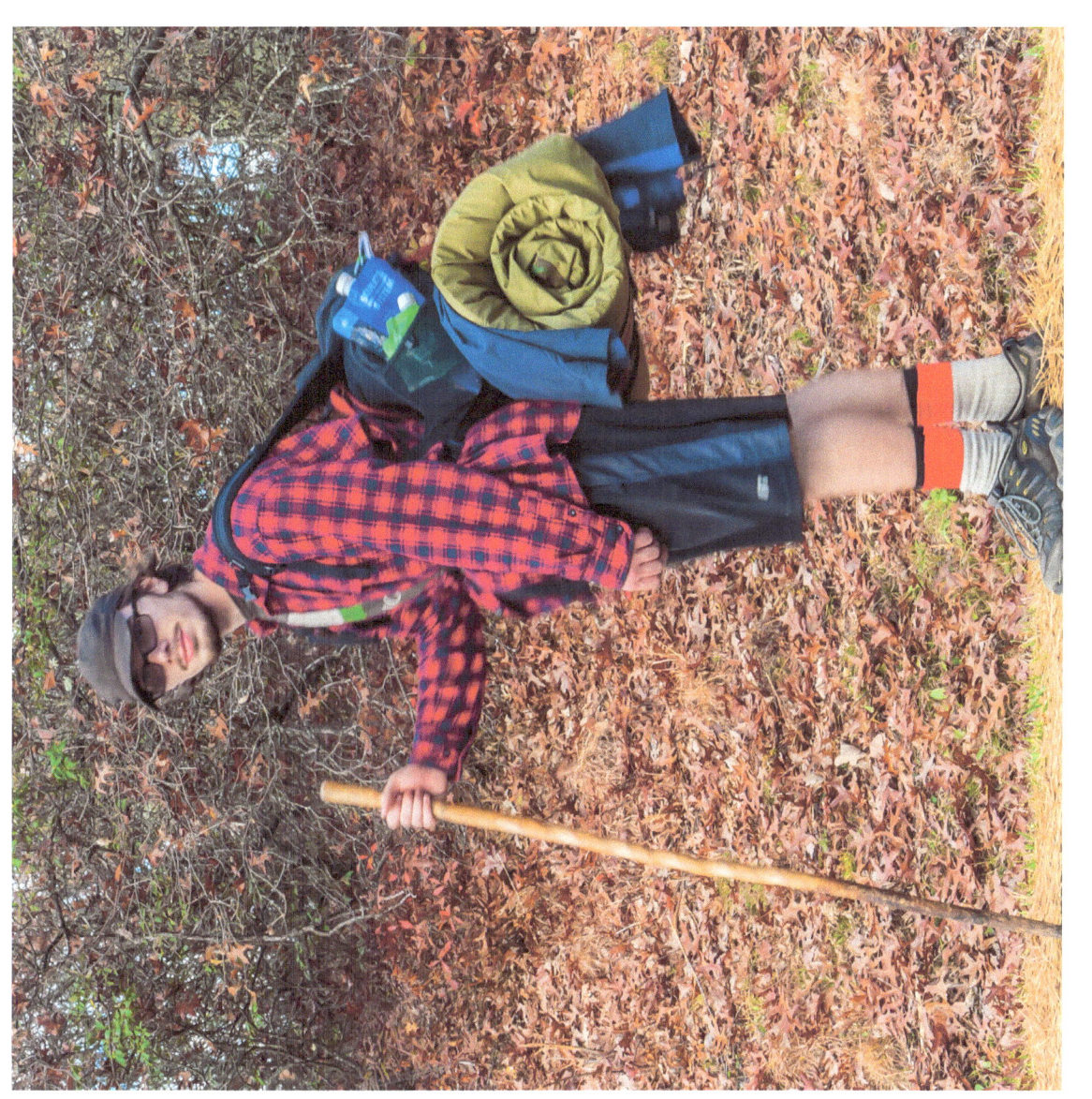

Hiker - Sawmill Run Overlook (2195 ft.)

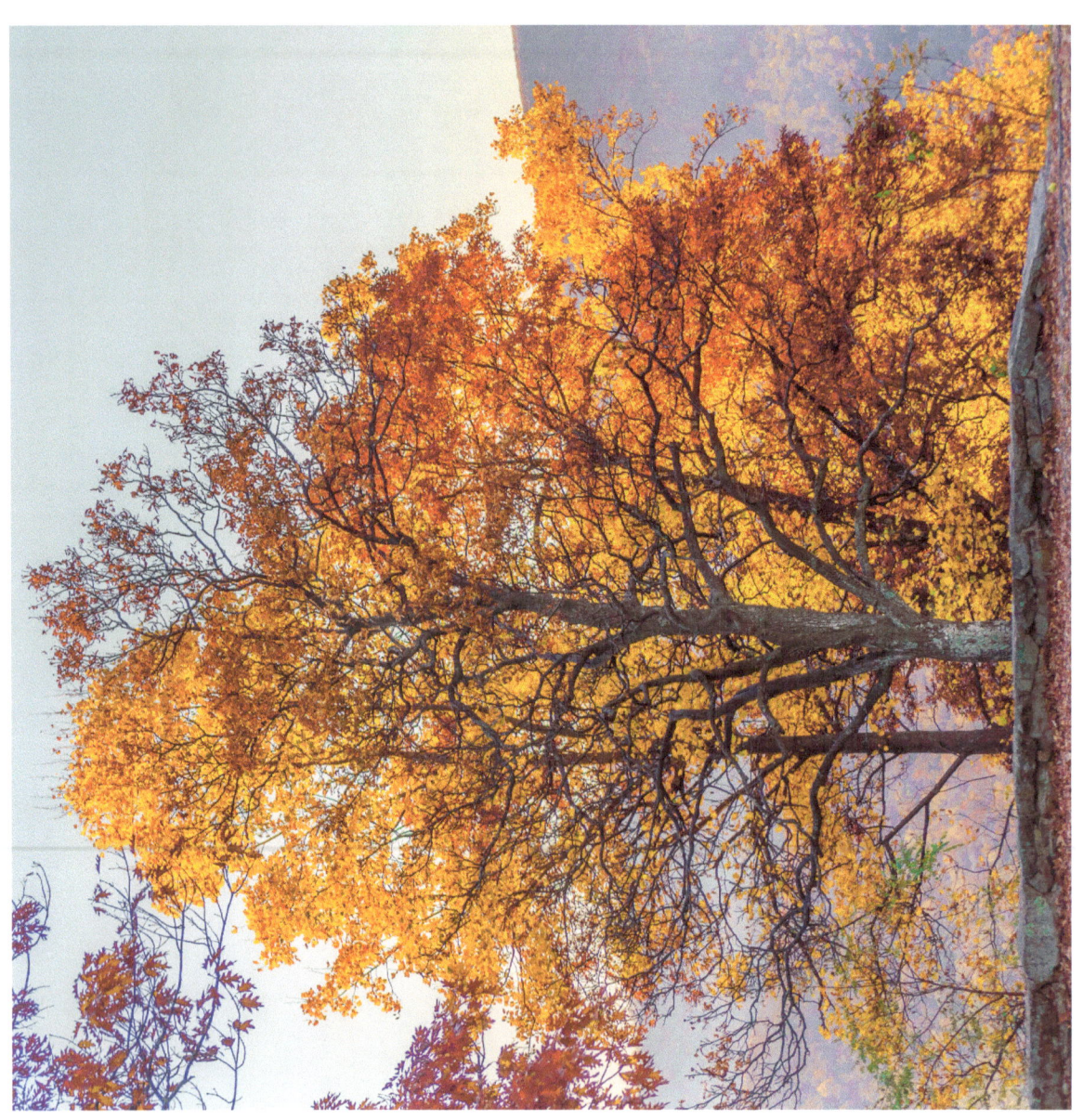

Foliage of Autumn Forest - Gooney Run Overlook (2085 ft.)

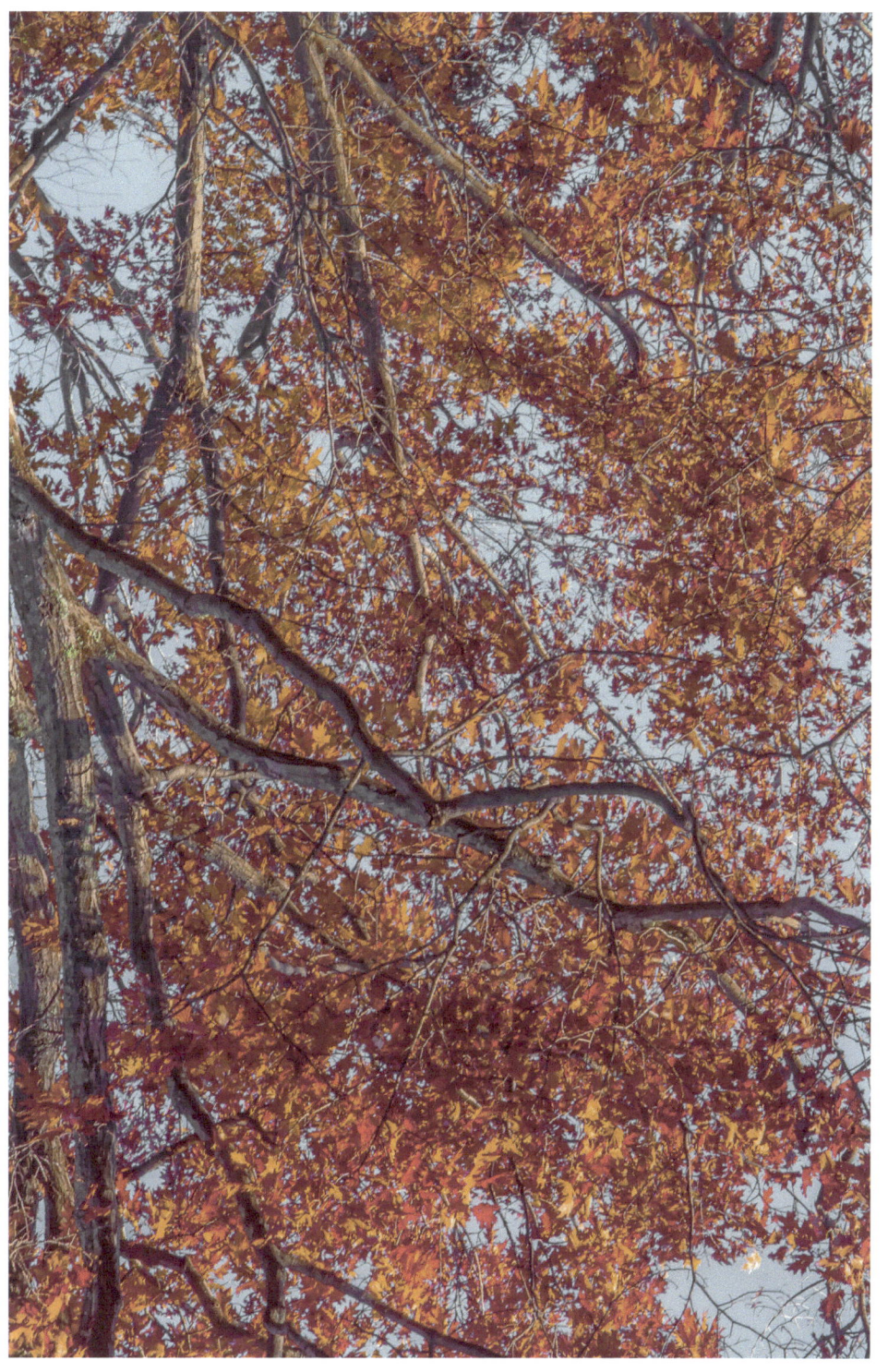

3-D Branches with Fall Leaves - Compton Gap Overlook (2415 ft.)

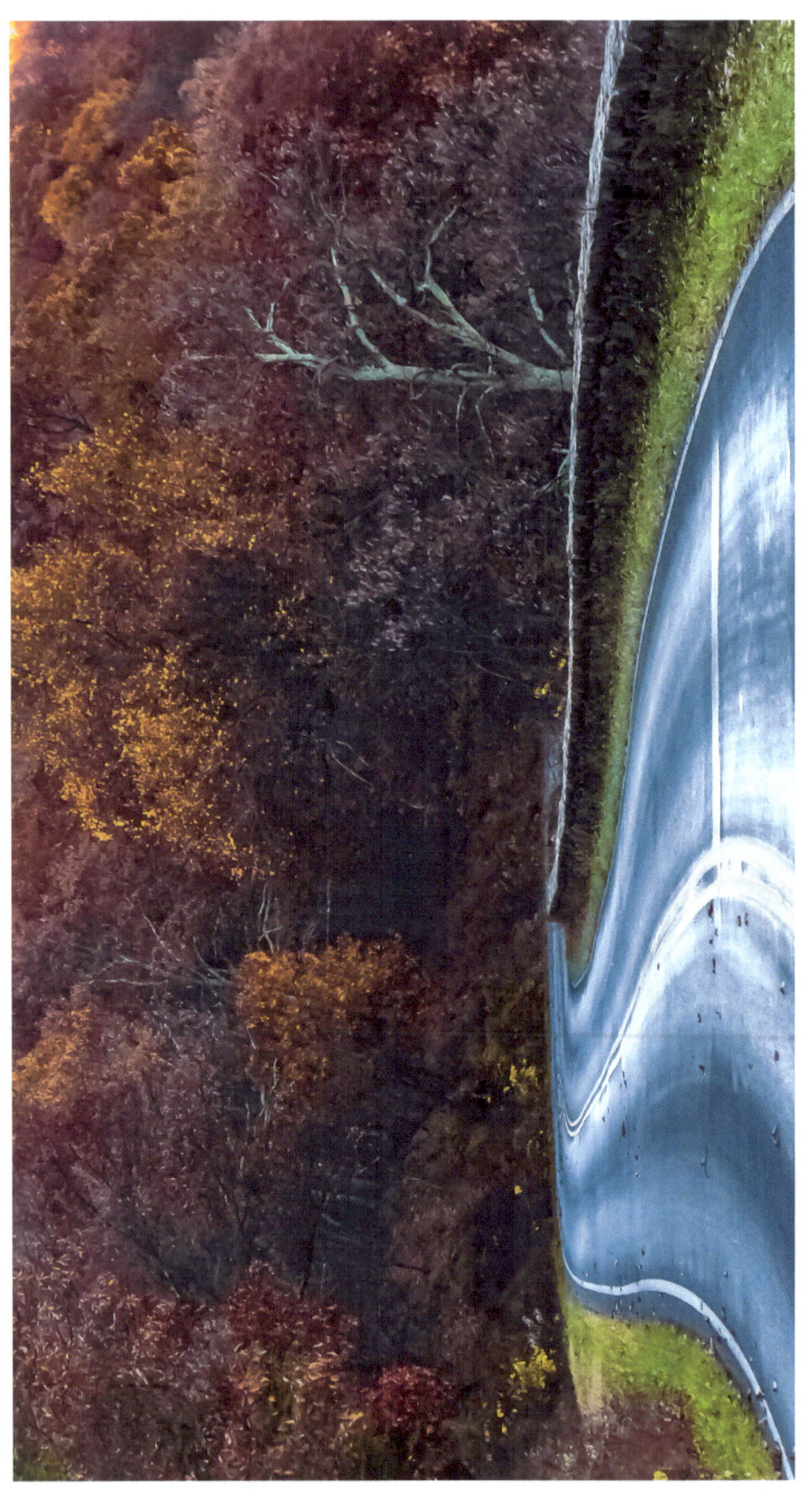

Coming 'Round the Bend - Gooney Run Overlook (2085 ft.)

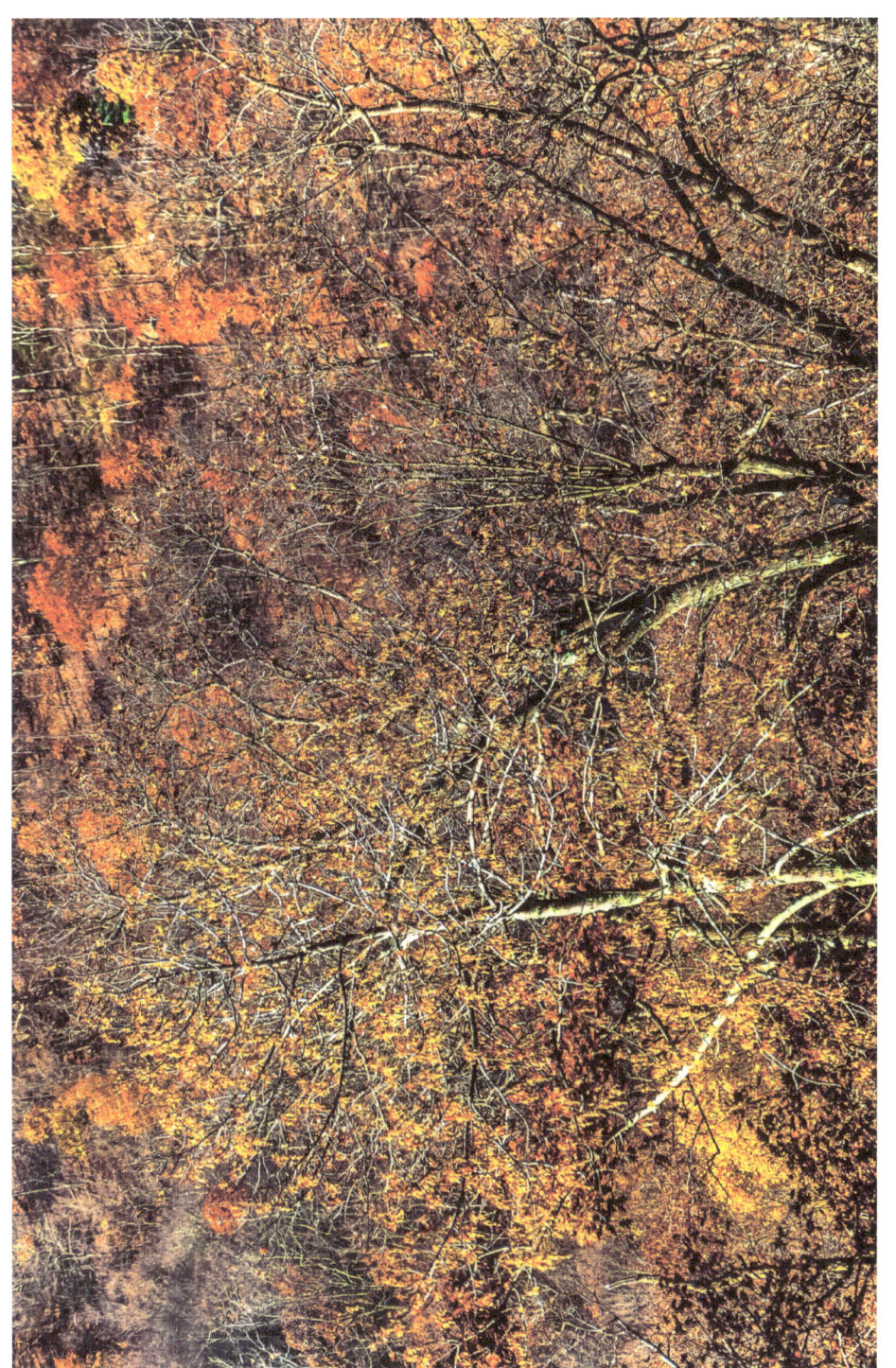

Dying Trees and a Collage of Yellow Tones- Franklin Cliffs Overlook (3140 ft.)

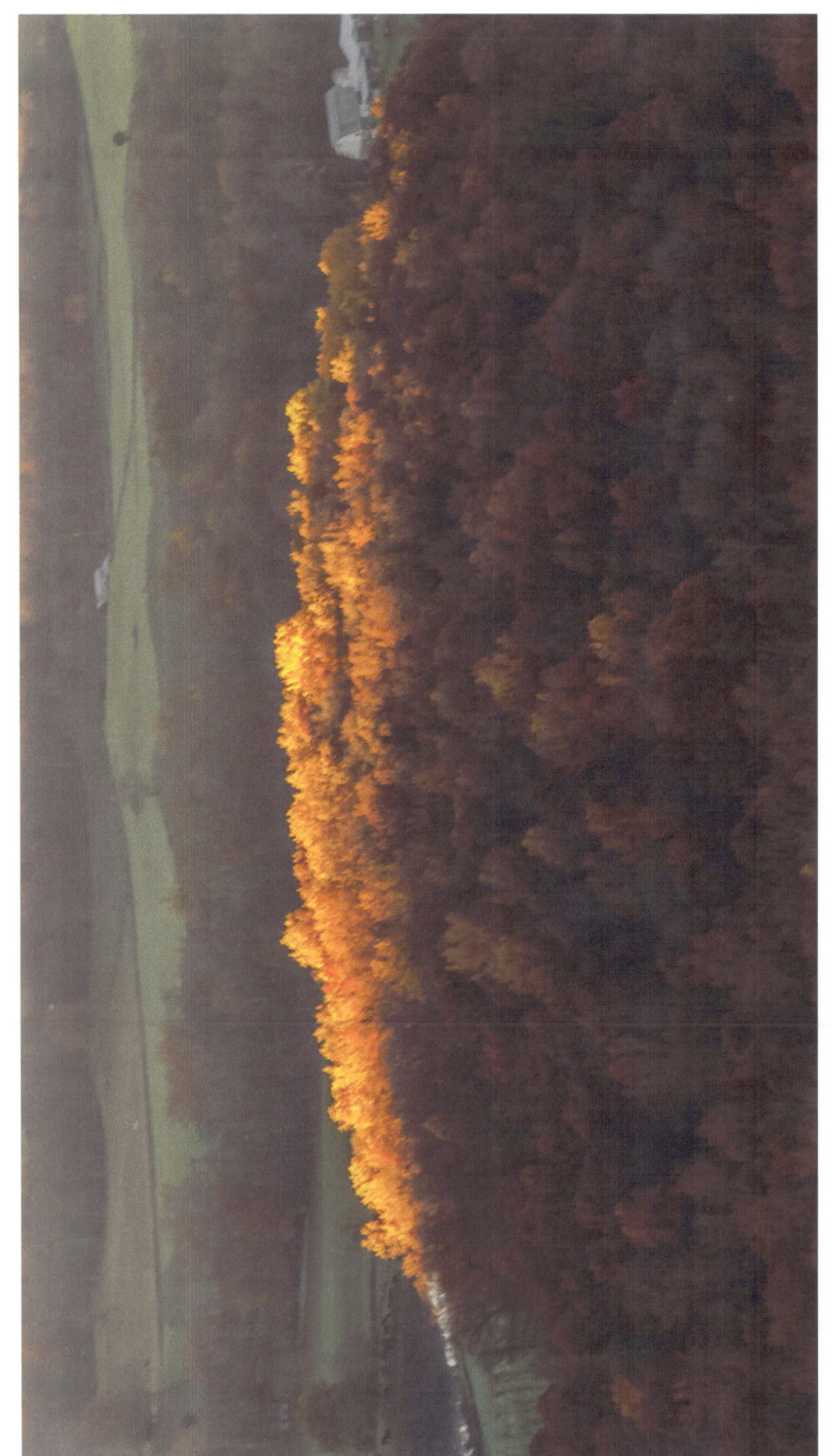

A Collage of Yellow Tones with Quality of Light - Gooney Manor Overlook (1920 ft.)

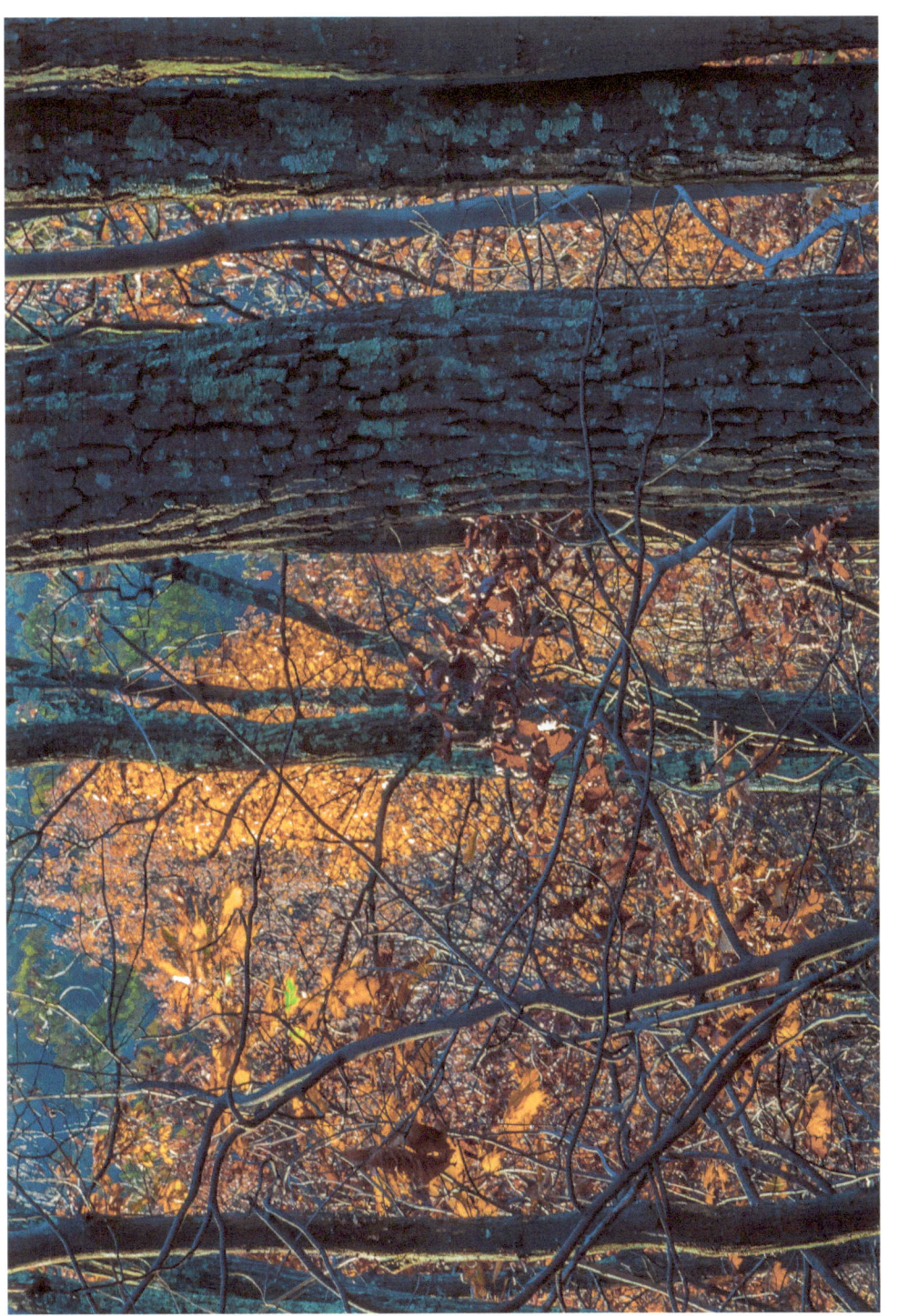

Colorful Green Algae on Tree Bark - Gooney Manor Overlook (1920 ft.)

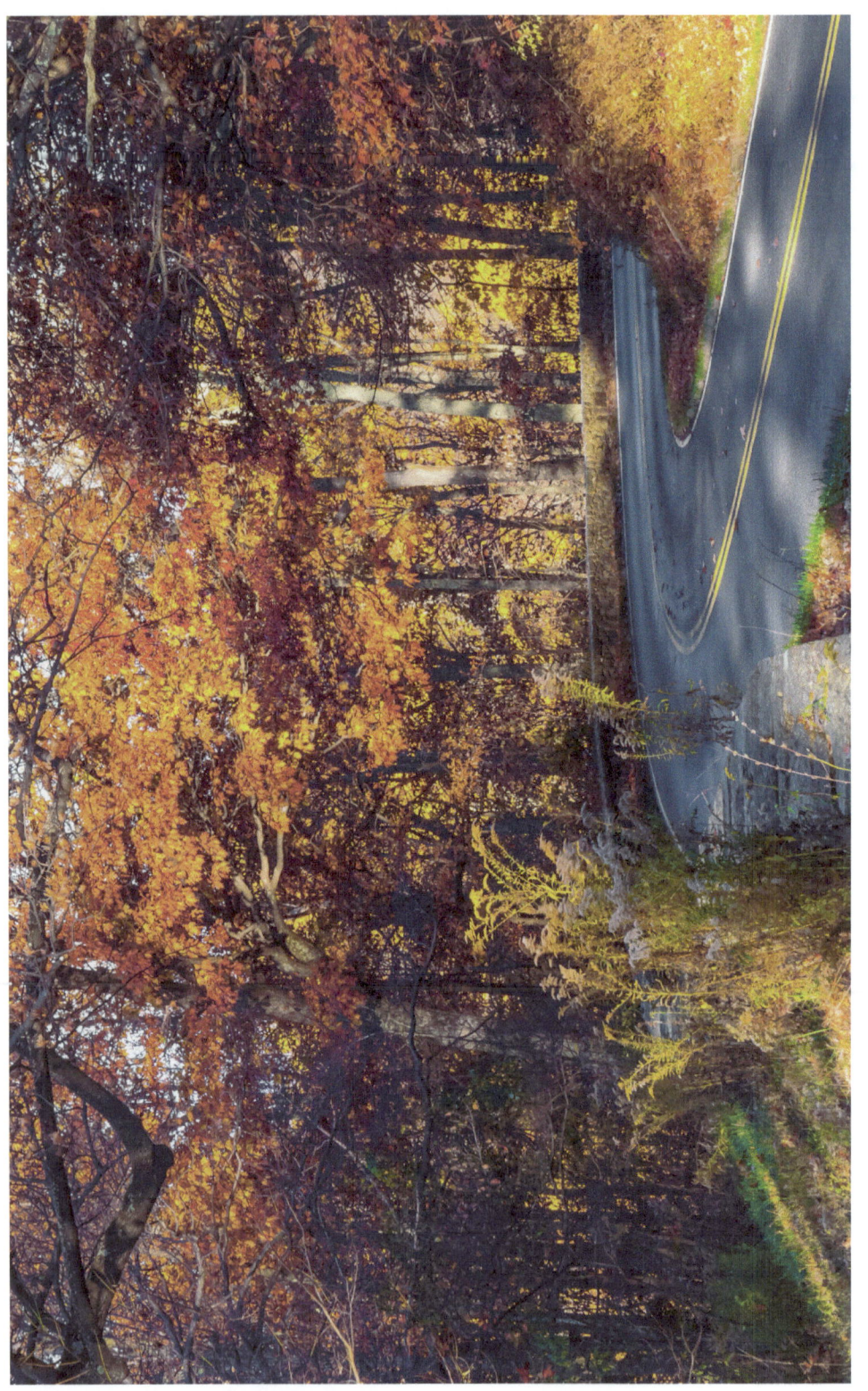

Fall Foliage in the Shenandoah Valley - Gooney Manor Overlook (1920 ft.)

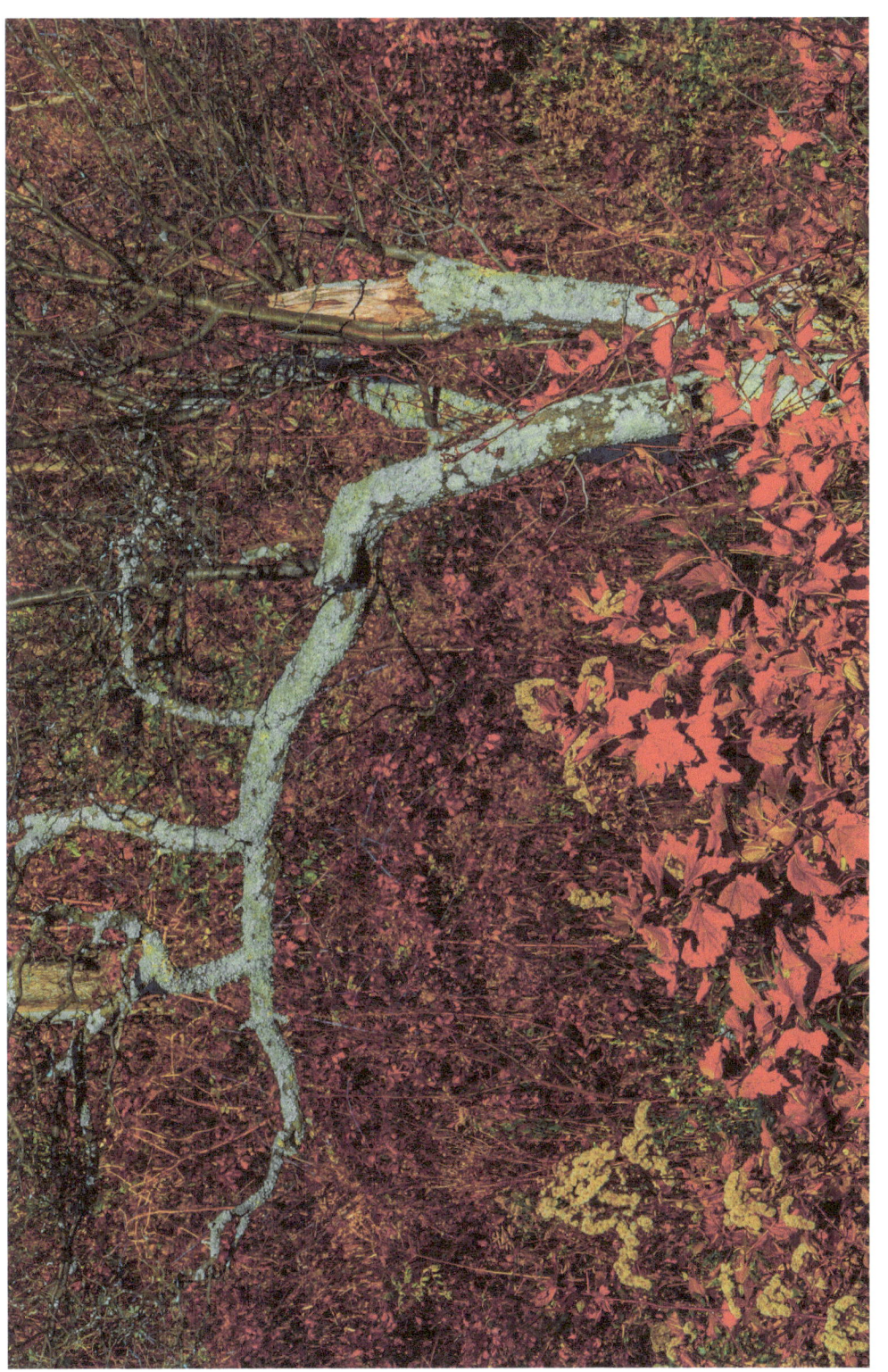

Leafless Tree Branch Art Resembling Antlers - Hogwallow Flats Overlook (2665 ft.)

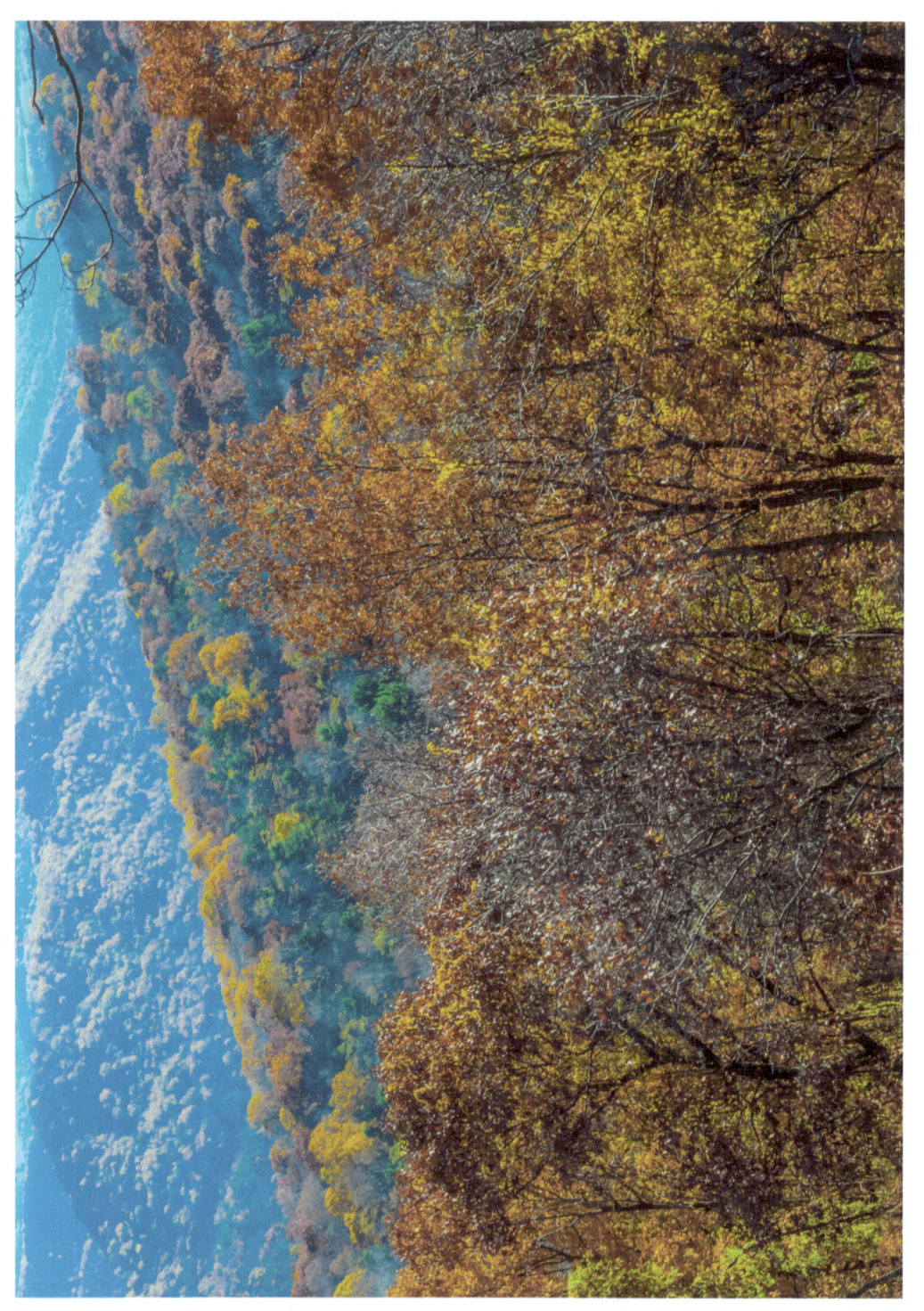

Autumn Leaves - Thornton Hollow Overlook (2460 ft.)

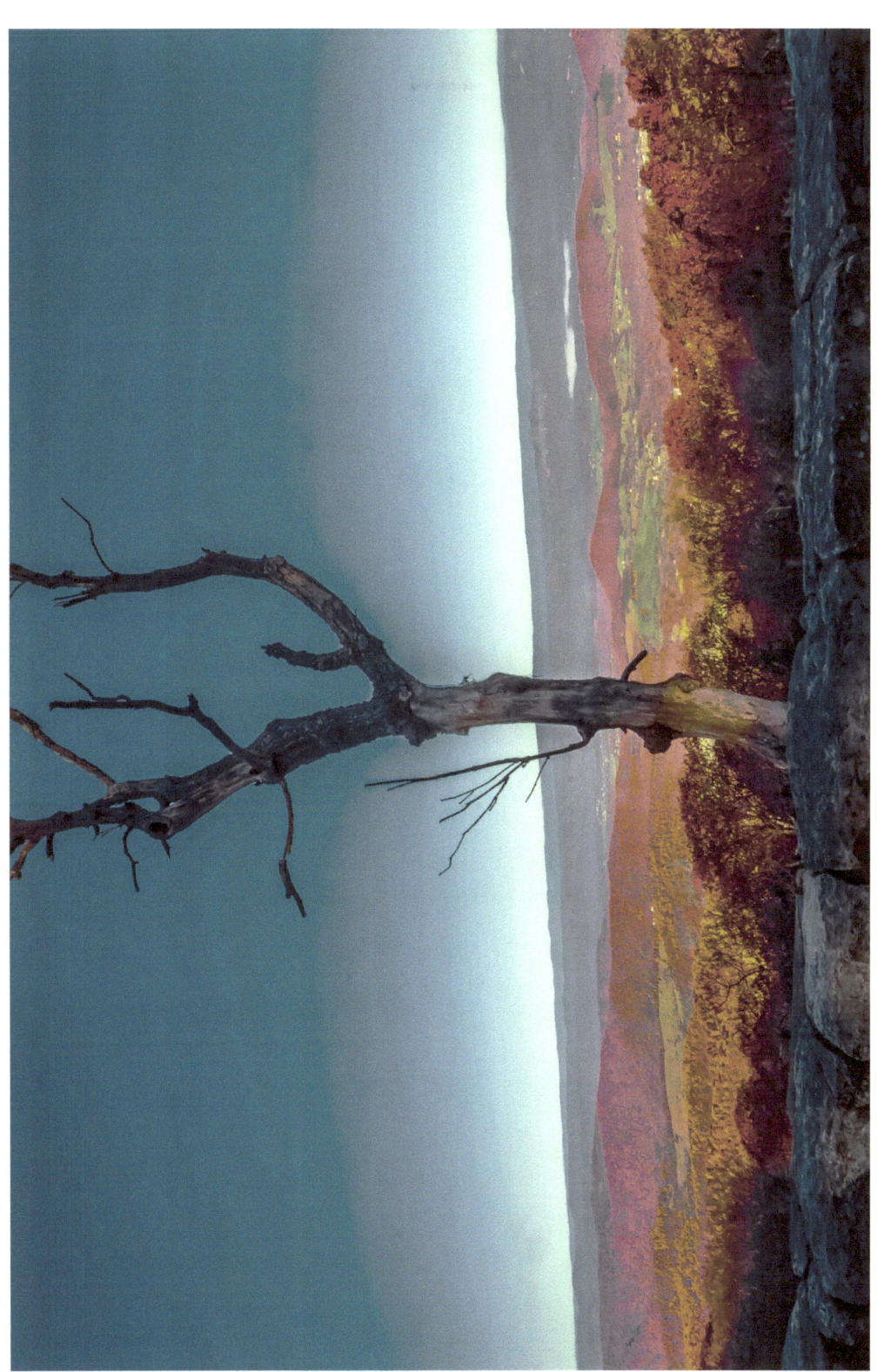

Autumn Naked Tree - Browntown Valley Overlook (2890 ft.)

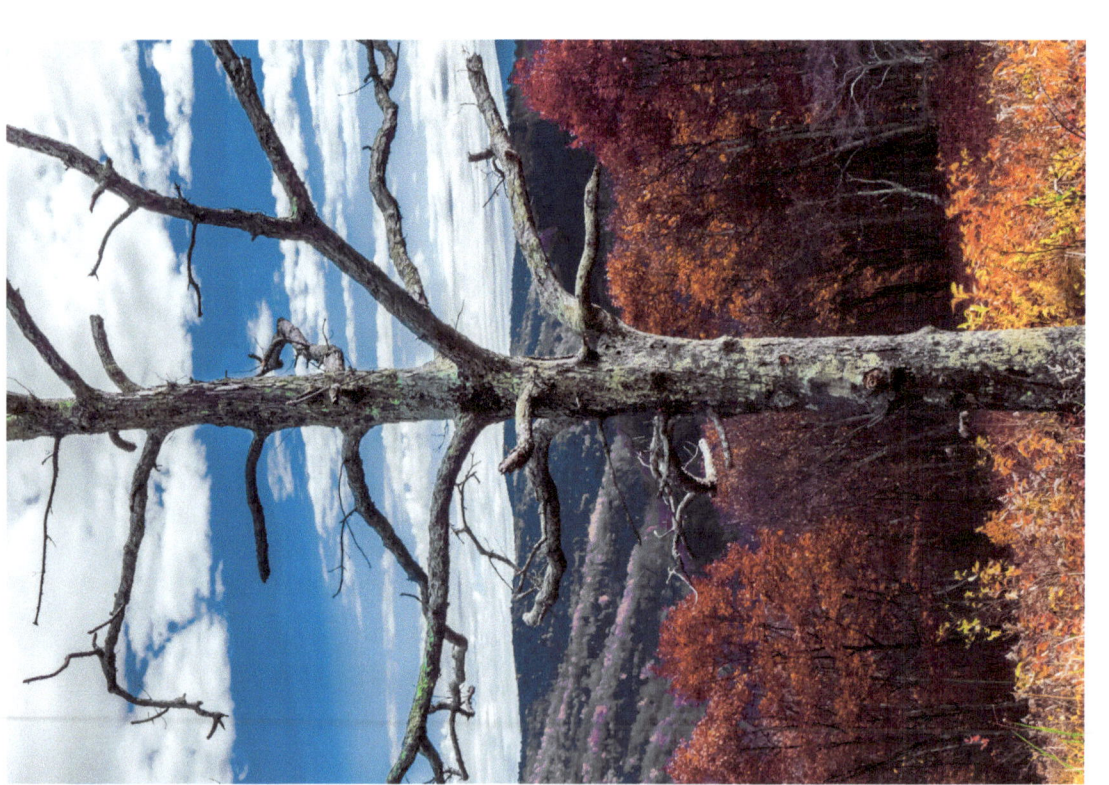

Leafless Tree Among Scenic Landscape 2 - Trayfoot Mountain Overlook (2575 ft.)

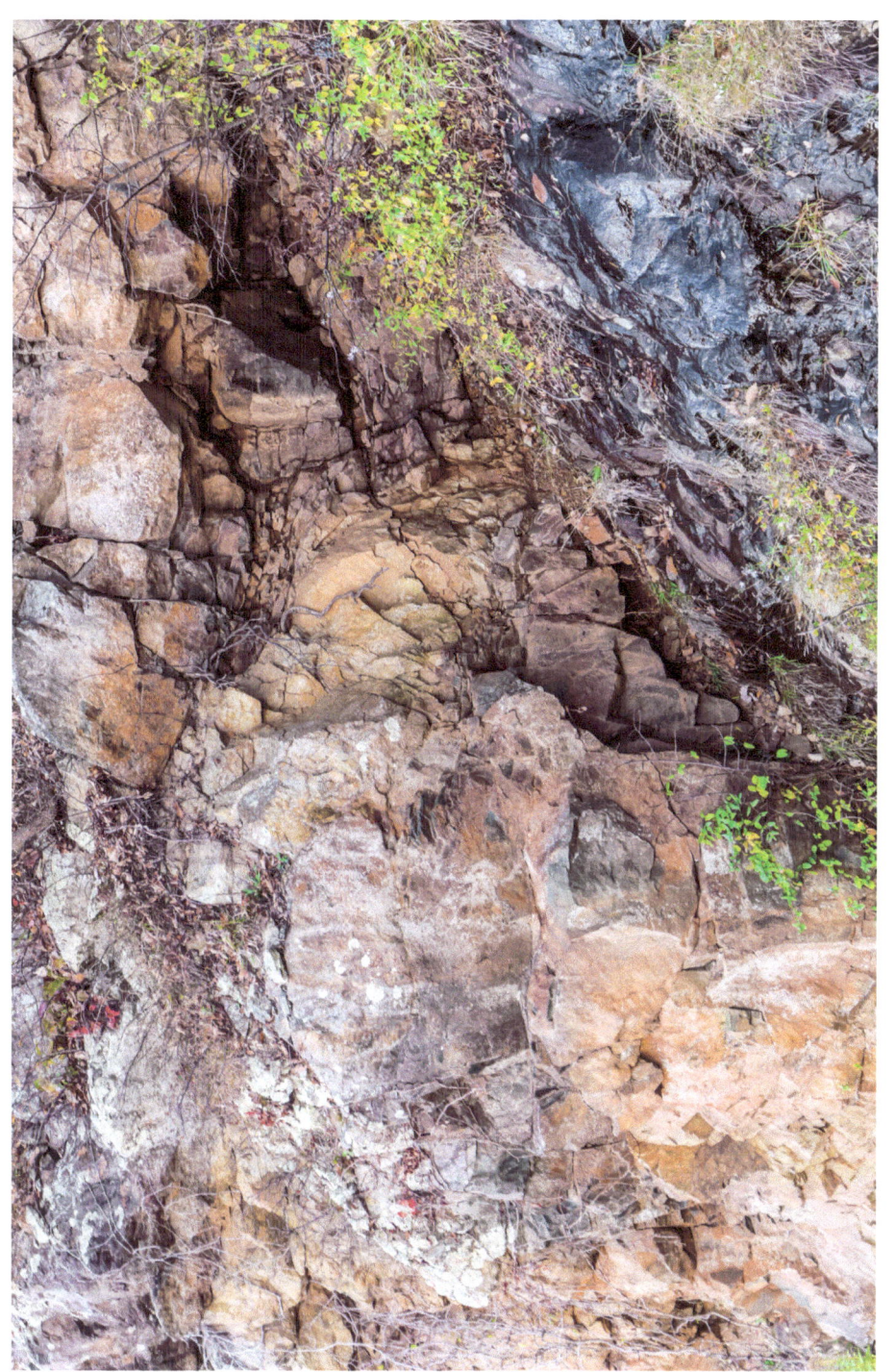

Geological Rock Types - Shenandoah Valley Overlook (1390 ft.)

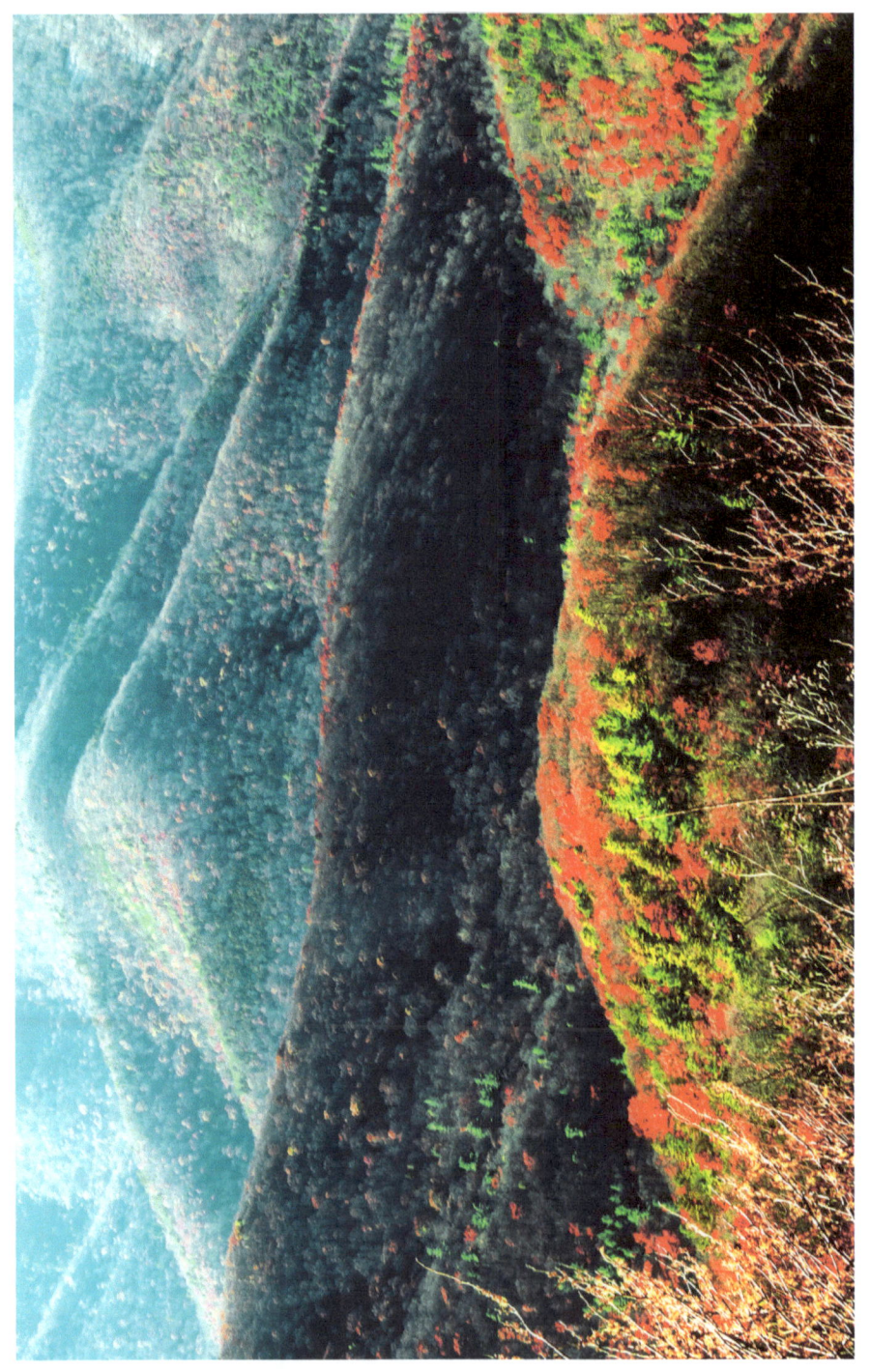

Mountain Peaks - Rockytop Overlook (2860 ft.)

Index

Symbols

3-D Branches with Fall Leaves - Compton Gap Overlook (2415 ft.) 35

A

A Beautiful Shenandoah Landscape - Shenandoah Valley Overlook (1390 ft.) 29
A Collage of Yellow Tones with Quality of Light - Gooney Manor Overlook (1920 ft.) 38
Algae 39
A Path Through a Rock Wall - Crescent Rock Overlook (3550 ft.) 13
Autumn 22, 24, 34, 40, 42, 43
Autumn Leaves - Thornton Hollow Overlook (2450 ft.) 40
Autumn Leaves - Thornton Hollow Overlook (2460 ft.) 42
Autumn Naked Tree - Browntown Valley Overlook (2890 ft.) 43

B

Beagle Gap 7
Bicyclist 1
Blowing Mountain Leaves - Mount Marshall Overlook (2850 ft.) 31
Brave Man on Rock - Hazel Mountain Overlook (2770 ft.) 11
Browntown Valley Overlook (2890 ft.) 43

C

Calf Mountain Overlook (2485 ft.) 7
Collage 37, 38
Colorful Green Algae on Tree Bark - Gooney Manor Overlook (1920 ft.) 39
Colorful Tree Tops - Trayfoot Mountain Overlook (2575 ft.) 25
Coming 'Round the Bend - Gooney Run Overlook (2085 ft.) 36
Compton Gap Overlook (2415 ft.) 35
Crescent Rock Overlook (3550 ft.) 13, 15

D

Dying Trees and a Collage of Yellow Tones- Franklin Cliffs Overlook (3140 ft.) 37

E

Elevation 20

F

Fall Foliage 1, 6
Foggy Mountain Scene - Shenandoah Valley Overlook (1390 ft.) 26
Foliage 1, 5, 6, 23, 34
Foliage of Autumn Forest - Gooney Run Overlook (2085 ft.) 34
Franklin Cliffs Overlook (3140 ft.) 37
ft. 1, 2, 3, 4, 5, 6, 7, 8, 9, 10, 11, 12, 13, 14, 15, 16, 17, 20, 21, 22, 23, 24, 25, 26, 27, 28, 29, 30, 31, 32, 33, 34, 35, 36, 37, 38, 39, 40, 41, 42, 43, 44, 45, 46

G

Geological Rock Types - Shenandoah Valley Overlook (1390 ft.) 45
Gooney Manor Overlook (1920 ft.) 6, 38, 39
Gooney Run Overlook (2085 ft.) 4, 5, 34, 36
Green Mountain Tree 30
Green Mountain Tree Showcases the Hazel Mountains - Hazel Mountain Overlook (2770 ft.) 30

H

Hazel Mountain Overlook (2770 ft.) 11, 30
Hiker 33
Hiker - Sawmill Run Overlook (2195 ft.) 33
Hogback Overlook (3385 ft.) 14, 28
Hogwallow Flats Overlook (2665 ft.) 9, 41
Horsehead Overlook (2575 ft.) 10, 32

L

Landscape 3, 24, 28, 29, 44
Landscape Autumn 24
Landscape Autumn - Shenandoah Valley Overlook (1390 ft.) 24
Leafless Tree 3, 41, 44
Leafless Tree Among Scenic Landscape 1 3
Leafless Tree Among Scenic Landscape 2 - Trayfoot Mountain Overlook (2575 ft.) 44
Leafless Tree Branch Art Resembling Antlers 41
Leafless Tree Branch Art Resembling Antlers - Hogwallow Flats Overlook (2665 ft.) 41
Leafless Trees 32
Leafless Trees and Vector Mountain - Horsehead Overlook (2575 ft.) 32
Leaves 31, 35, 40, 42
Lookouts 1, ii
Luray, Virginia ii, 20

M

Mary's Rock Tunnel Side Wall - Tunnel Parking Overlook (2840 ft.) 21
McCormick Gap Overlook (2455 ft.) 17
Mobile Visitor Center 19
Mobile Visitor Center at Shenandoah National Park- Wayside Comfort Station 19
Mountain ii, 3, 7, 11, 17, 22, 25, 26, 27, 30, 31, 32, 44, 46

Mountain Peaks 46
Mountain Peaks - Rockytop Overlook (2860 ft.) 46
Mount Marshall Overlook (2850 ft.) 16, 31

N

Naked Tree 43
Natural Geometric Forms - Hogwallow Flats Overlook (2665 ft.) 9

O

Old Rag View Overlook (3585 ft.) 2
Overlook 1, 2, 3, 4, 5, 6, 7, 8, 9, 10, 11, 12, 13, 14, 15, 16, 17, 21, 22, 23, 24, 25, 26, 27, 28, 29, 30, 31, 32, 33, 34, 35, 36, 37, 38, 39, 40, 41, 42, 43, 44, 45, 46

P

Pass Mountain Overlook (2460 ft.) 27

Q

Quality of Light 8, 38
Quality of Light with Complementary Colors 8

R

Ranger 18
Ranger Displays Literature and Artifacts at Wayside Comfort Station 18
Restroom Accessibility at Beagle Gap - Calf Mountain Overlook (2485 ft.) 7
Rock 11, 13, 14, 15, 21, 45
Rock and Tree Wall - Crescent Rock Overlook (3550 ft.) 15
Rock Stone 14
Rock Stone Texture on Rock Wall - Hogback Overlook (3385 ft.) 14
Rocky Pathways - Horsehead Overlook (2575 ft.) 10
'Round the Mountain on Skyline Drive - Pass Mountain Overlook (2460 ft.) 27

S

Sawmill Ridge Overlook (2210 ft.) 12
Sawmill Run Overlook (2195 ft.) 1, 33
Scenic Landscape 3, 44
Scenic Vista - Sawmill Ridge Overlook (2210 ft.) 12
Shenandoah National Park 1, ii, iv, 19
Shenandoah Valley Foliage 5
Shenandoah Valley Foliage - Gooney Run Overlook 5
Shenandoah Valley Overlook (1390 ft.) 8, 23, 24, 26, 29, 45
Shirley Nan Washington, Ed.D. 1
Skyland Resort 20
Skyland Resort in Luray, Virginia - The Highest Point of Elevation on Skyline Drive (3680 ft.) 20
Skyline Drive ii, iv, 20, 23, 27
Skyline Drive Foliage View - Shenandoah Valley Overlook (1390 ft.) 23
Spectacular Landscape View - Hogback Overlook (3385 ft.) 28
Sunrise Trees 4
Sunrise Trees - Gooney Run Overlook (2085 ft.) 4

T

The Quintessential Look of Autumn - Thorofare Mountain Overlook (3595 ft.) 22
Thick Tree Bark with Growing Moss on Tree 2
Thornton Hollow Overlook (2450 ft.) 40
Thornton Hollow Overlook (2460 ft.) 42
Thorofare Mountain Overlook (3595 ft.) 22
Trayfoot Mountain Overlook (2575 ft.) 3, 25, 44
Tree Bark 2, 39
Tree Framed Mountain View - McCormick Gap Overlook (2455 ft.) 17
Tree Shadows 16
Tree Shadows on Rocks - Mount Marshall Overlook (2850 ft.) 16
Tunnel Parking Overlook (2840 ft.) 21

V

Vector Mountain 32

W

Waynesboro, Virginia 1
Waynesboro, Virginia Bicyclist 1
Wayside Comfort Station 18, 19

Y

Yellow-Orange Fall Foliage - Gooney Manor Overlook (1920 ft.) 6

www.ingramcontent.com/pod-product-compliance
Lightning Source LLC
Chambersburg PA
CBHW051216220526
45473CB00003B/1055